VIBE

$E=RF^2$

Energy Equals RESULTS Faster Squared

TONY JEARY
THE RESULTS GUY™

WITH DANIEL MAROLD, COO

Vibe

Published by RESULTS Faster Publishing in association with Clovercroft Publishing, Franklin, Tennessee

Editing by Adept Content Solutions

Cover Design by Brooke Hawkins

Interior Design by Adept Content Solutions

Printed in the United States of America

ISBN: 978-1-950892-96-9

CONTENTS

***Note:** This book addresses Vibe in relation to two entities—the individual and the organization. The chapter headings are separated by a slash. The first part applies to the individual, and the second part applies to the organization.*

LETTER FROM SCOTT BENNETT

It has been fifteen years since I first met Tony Jeary; a high school friend had made the introduction. Ron said anyone in the investment business should know Tony. Ron was right. Shortly after our first meeting I hired Tony to help vet a business concept. After a day's long session with Tony, I realized I would never undertake a business venture without bringing my team together for a day in Tony's studio.

As a one-time and long-time journalist, I am a trained skeptic. I don't believe anything without evidence. Trust but definitely verify. Tony was no different. I was told that he had a magic ability to bring teams whose members were at each other's throats together, marching in unison. I was told that he had the ability to find value others couldn't see and to find ways to get things done that others could not find. I was told that he could infuse the most moribund organization with energy and enthusiasm. And guess what? I have personally seen him do all those things.

Put another way: Tony has the *Vibe.* What I mean by "vibe" is that every area of Tony's life, personal and professional, vibrates with results-driven energy. And it shows. It shows in his RESULTS Center office building where every detail is architected to help visiting clients achieve their goal-driven results. Tony's vibe comes across in his family, in his personality, and in his employees. It's like an energy beam hit a tuning fork and created the winning vibe.

I hesitate to use the word *unique* because that means one of a kind. But I can say that I have met many of Tony's clients, and they have all used the word unique. Part of his magic is process. He has been in the business of driving results for forty years, and he knows what works and what doesn't. Part of the magic is a positive "the answer is out there" mindset that is still realistic enough to admit when it is not out there.

Tony has been executive coach to the best and the neophyte. He has learned what trips leaders up and what it takes to make it. He has worked with organizations such as Walmart and Chrysler. He has also spent hundreds of hours with startups showing them the path to becoming a Walmart.

Tony has also published books providing strategic guidance, such as his bestselling *Life is a Series of Presentations* and *Strategic Acceleration*. He has published dozens of guides focused on such micro subjects as how to hold meetings that accomplish something and managing email. The time saved in doing those small things efficiently adds up fast. Tony says he can give any executive an extra hour a day, and that is not an idle boast.

All these books, all these ideas, add up to something larger. They create something. But I have never been able to say exactly what they created. That fell to Tony's colleague and protégé, Daniel Marold, COO. Daniel calls it a "vibe." I agree. We are not talking about packaging; all that is a part of the story. A vibe is something far more substantive that reveals inner reality.

Tony and Daniel have taken a welcome step by pulling together their strategies, methods, and best practices for achieving a vibe in both the individual and organization. I highly recommend *Vibe* as a resource for you and your organization. There is a lot of insight and a lot of just common sense in this thoughtful book. But, as the CEO of a FORTUNE 10 company said while listening to one of Tony's presentations, "We don't DO any of this and we should be doing all of it." You should too.

Scott Bennett
Partner, Mobility Ventures

INTRODUCTION

Remember the Beach Boys song "Good Vibrations?" Or perhaps you recall the movie *Kelly's Heroes* where the hippie tank commander called Oddball (played by Donald Sutherland) was always berating his crew for "bad vibes." If your memory doesn't stretch back that far, you have certainly walked into a restaurant or a club or even a home and thought to yourself, "What a great vibe."

So what is this vibe that seems to be so important? According to the dictionary, it is an emotional reaction to the aura felt to belong to a person, place, or thing. An *aura* is "a distinctive atmosphere surrounding a given source."

For purposes of this book, the given source is either you or your organization. The goal is to give off good vibes and not negative vibes. You want to make people go "Wow, this is someone I want to be around" or "This is a company I want to do business with."

People sometimes react to this concept as a bit akin to buying a book by its cover or a bottle of wine by its label. And they are exactly right, because people do buy books by their covers and wine by its label. A label design for a new vintage of wine can start at $100,000 and soar to $1 million. Even connoisseurs are influenced in their purchases by the label design.

How do you create a vibe? Energy. Building your vibe or your company's vibe is sort of like painting by numbers. There are lots of separate items that make up the picture. But what puts those items together, what makes a vibe more than just a façade, is energy. Energy is what makes the presentation into the reality.

Vibe doesn't mean making everyone into Tom Brady. Albert Einstein had the perfect vibe for who he was: the pipe, the rumpled sweater, the moustache, the frizzy white hair. Einstein projected in every way the vibe of a brilliant physicist who was nevertheless an approachable, homespun man. Yet, Einstein's vibe was powered by the energy of a powerful mind.

For an organizational vibe there is no better example than Susan B. Komen for the Cure. Its pink ribbon logo forms the shape of a runner. Its global run for the cure became its signature activity. The Komen Foundation was created by Susan Komen's younger sister, Nancy. Nancy Koman Brinker took care that every aspect of the organization created a vibe composed of life, health, action, and energy. She wanted to communicate to the victims of breast cancer and their loved ones that there was hope and that hope came through the energy of millions of dedicated people from researchers to eighty-year-old cancer survivors running for their cure.

For nearly forty years, Tony Jeary International has worked with the best organizations in America to help them achieve mastery. We have worked with the world's leading companies to take them to the top level. We could certainly tell you what steps you had to take to get to mastery or build your company's market value, yet we struggled to explain exactly what it was we were trying to create. Then one day, Daniel suggested we were trying to create the right vibe.

Vibe resonated with me. Vibe, we realized, wasn't just an outward manifestation; it wasn't just the car you drove or the house you lived in but everything that composed your life that said you had it together—your friends, your principles, your family, your comfort in your own skin. You can't fake your vibe, at least not for very long. As important as a first impression is, if it isn't real, it will fade away. A vibe is a vibe because it reflects reality. Companies are no different, just more complex.

Had Einstein attempted to create a Babe Ruth vibe, he would have been a joke. Can you imagine Tom Brady with an Einstein vibe? Either would have been fake and funny. A vibe has to be natural and real. Creating a powerful vibe is like taking an old pair of shoes to a master shiner. When you get them back, all of the original quality stands out. They glow. People who see them want to know where you got them. That's vibe. But the natural vibe was brought out by the energy of the cobbler who made them and the shine artists who restored them.

What Daniel and I want to do in this book is to explain how you build and shine your life and your business to a high-energy vibe. There aren't any big secrets here. No complicated Harvard Business Review strategies. The building blocks are simple, though some will have you slapping your head and saying, "of course!" Our intent isn't to dazzle it. Our intent is to help you realize how all the small pieces build on each other to create a credible (maybe an incredible) vibe.

PART 1
BRAND

"A brand is not so much about rational arguments, but the way that the company resonates with people emotionally."
—Steve Jobs

Most people associate the word "brand" with the word "reputation." In fact, Jeff Bezos has said, "Your brand is what other people say about you when you're not in the room." Both your brand and your reputation precede you.

You're aware that brand matters, of course, because you know people make judgments based on brand. You may not be aware that every brand radiates a *Vibe* at a subconscious level that's either attractive or repulsive.

EVERY BRAND RADIATES SOME KIND OF VIBE—AN ENERGY AT A SUBCONSCIOUS LEVEL THAT'S EITHER IRRESISTIBLE OR REPULSIVE.

In this section, we show how to be intentional in making your brand's *Vibe* so irresistible that people will want to do business with you, work with you, or strategically partner with you. You want to purposely create a *Vibe* that reveals that you care about people and want them to win. You can't accomplish this in just one way. It requires utilizing every platform available to you: your website, LinkedIn, and your entire online presence. Do you have Yelp reviews? Have your ex-employees posted reviews on Glass Door? Has anyone filed a lawsuit against you? You would be amazed at what is online. All these channels are extensions of your brand, which means people can actually access the *Vibe* that exudes from your brand and you can build rapport with them before they even meet you or set foot in your organization's space.

Most people don't consciously register their impression of how they feel when they encounter someone's brand. However, they sense whether energy and excitement exists, and *Vibe* (or lack of it) serves as the subconscious influencer about whether to take the next step. For instance, when corporate executives consider leasing space in an office park I own, they'll often look at the website first and then talk to people who are already leasing there. They're subconsciously looking for the *Vibe* that will help them determine whether they want to consider meeting with the leasing agent to establish their business in the park.

Whether you're an entrepreneur, in sales, a leader, someone growing your résumé, a partner, a professional, an influencer, or a top executive in an organization, you have to decide to be strategic about building a brand with exceptional *Vibe*.

CHAPTER 1
OPEN AND GROWING/ INNOVATIVE

For the Individual Leader: Open and Growing

One of the most powerful books dealing with success I've ever read is Dale Carnegie's *How to Win Friends and Influence People.* My girlfriend's father gave a copy to me when I was sixteen, and it was life changing. (Certain books can have that effect—they can change your life.) In the book, Carnegie gives thirty principles to live by, and most are about being open, listening, and caring about other people. Openness is a quality that adds *Vibe* to your personal brand.

OPENNESS IS A QUALITY THAT ADDS VIBE TO YOUR PERSONAL LEADERSHIP BRAND.

A company we had been helping for about a year needed a CEO. Out of thousands of my personal contacts, I picked an executive who seemed a fit. I invited him to come to the RESULTS Center to meet the founders and some of the partners. When he arrived, he exuded a remarkable *Vibe.* His personal presentation was perfect for the occasion. Even more notable was that he invested the first half hour listening before he said anything about himself. When he did speak, he exhibited the traits of an exceptional leader—one who is open to hearing, exploring, and understanding by asking questions like "What's important to you?" and "What is your vision?"

To enhance your *Vibe* by growing the trait of openness, I highly recommend you read Carnegie's book, along with Stephen R. Covey's *The 7 Habits of Highly Effective People*, which includes a chapter on the habit of seeking first to understand.

A component of openness is curiosity. When you develop a strong sense of curiosity, you will likely become a lifelong learner, and you will begin to surround yourself with learning materials such as books, videos, links, and podcasts. By doing so, you create a double win.

1. You expand your knowledge and expertise as you constantly expose your mind to new information.
2. You enhance your brand's *Vibe* by showing you're open to growing and learning.

A COMPONENT OF OPENNESS IS CURIOSITY. YOU ENHANCE YOUR BRAND'S VIBE BY SHOWING YOU'RE OPEN TO GROWING AND LEARNING.

Seeking advice from mentors who have been successful in areas where you want to grow is another way to learn and grow. I often talk about my coach, Mark Pantact, whom I've had for three decades, and my mentors because it shows that my brand includes being open and constantly searching for feedback. When I tell people that I meet a couple of times a month for two or three hours on a Sunday afternoon with my eighty-year-old business mentor, Jay Rodgers, I get their attention. Jay and I coauthored a book a few years ago called *Advice Matters*, which talks about the urgency of seeking advice from others to get the results you want. By continually seeking advice from Jay and being open to uncovering my personal blind spots and gaining new perspectives, I practice what I preach. And since my colleague Daniel joined our organization as general manager, he and I meet together with Jay, which adds a unique dynamic. We achieve an *elegant solution* by simultaneously gleaning Jay's insight and building a stronger foundation by bringing three generations together in an open dialogue.

SEEKING ADVICE FROM MENTORS WHO HAVE BEEN SUCCESSFUL IN AREAS WHERE YOU WANT TO GROW IS ANOTHER WAY TO PROVE YOU'RE RECEPTIVE TO LEARNING AND GROWING.

How about you? Do people recognize the trait of openness in your brand?

For Your Organization: Innovative

What kind of *Vibe* does your organization emit in the area of innovation?

For example, are you open to bringing in subject-matter experts to supercharge the energy and thinking of your team? That doesn't necessarily involve paying large fees to name-brand experts, although that may be appropriate if the initiative is big enough. Sometimes, it's just a matter of bringing them in on a conference call or for an hour or so. Whether you're a CEO or other top executive or you lead a department, you want to be constantly seeking out expertise to bring innovative ideas and solutions to your strategic plan. If you don't have fresh ideas flowing in, you will become stuck in outdated practices that will cause you to lose your relevancy as well as your positive *Vibe.*

> Whether you're a CEO or other top executive or you lead a department, you want to be constantly seeking out expertise to bring innovative ideas and solutions to the business plan you're following. If you don't have fresh ideas flowing in, you could be stuck in outdated practices that will cause you to lose your relevancy as well as your positive *Vibe.*

Often, when people consider hiring subject-matter experts, they think of it as an expense rather than an investment. It does involve a bottom-line outgo, of course, yet there's a twist in the way you should think about it. Look at it through the lens of innovation and understand that you're investing in your people and making your plan happen faster. At times you may also be investing to avoid a risk. One of the offerings our agency brings to the table is risk mitigation. When people hire us to come into the organization, we look for innovative ways to protect them from risks they haven't seen.

The bullseye here is that you are bringing in mentors, coaches, and/or subject-matter experts who have expertise beyond what your organization has internally, with the aim of helping you be innovative, go for it, and be relevant.

You can often experience a company's *Vibe* by the innovative way it designs its workspace and serves its customers. For example, we've built as a physical location an innovative think tank called the RESULTS Center (RESULTSCenter.com) where we bring in top leaders and influencers from all over the world to develop strategies. The entire experience is designed so clients will encounter our *Vibe* by being fully immersed in it.

YOU CAN OFTEN EXPERIENCE A COMPANY'S VIBE BY THE INNOVATIVE WAY IT DESIGNS ITS WORKSPACE AND SERVES ITS CUSTOMERS.

The customers' experience starts at DFW Airport when the RESULTS1 Van picks them up. The interior of the van is designed to look like the interior of a private jet. This communicates speed (one of our key brand elements), innovation, and care for our clients' safety and comfort. They're dropped off in the hangar where the van is housed. Even this space is designed to create a *Vibe* of an organization that will make every minute of their time count while dealing with a company that prioritizes efficiency and structure. The hangar showcases vision-board best practices. As the customers walk toward the front of the building, they may see their company's name in our Floor of Fame. That's a brick paved area in the front of our building where we have engraved the names of the organizations whose presidents we have personally coached.

Over the top? People love it. It is a lighthearted way of showing appreciation while doing a little *Vibe* creation.

When they get inside the RESULTS Center, they can see we've devoted a segment of our space to a refreshment area called the Health Bar—named, of course, because it's filled with healthy food and drinks. We also keep a stock of books there to give away—books that impact lives in the area of health.

Oh, we've found that our guests are usually fascinated when we show them the six-inch concealed closet we've built near the Health Bar to house a special tabletop we can set on our bumper pool table when we want to convert it to a lunch table.

Inside the studio itself, our guests will find a wall-length cabinet that houses a more than thirty-year collection of best practices, which are all available to them. The studio is filled with customized furniture and innovative lighting, and there are plugins at each chair where all the team members can plug in their computers.

When we take them upstairs to the open-air lounge, where we serve lunch on nice days, visiting clients are surprised to find a deck and furniture that would rival that of a quality restaurant. Our goal is to always amaze people, and we have invested in such innovations as installing flooring pavers that stand four inches off the ground to provide instant drainage, which keeps the floor dry. Again, the *Vibe* gains depth: attention to detail and the best quality.

YOU CAN MAKE EVERY ASPECT OF YOUR SPACE SO INTENTIONAL THAT PEOPLE ARE ALREADY CAPTIVATED BY YOUR ENERGY BEFORE YOU EVEN WALK INTO THE ROOM.

Let's face it, most people don't react favorably when they are told they are flying across the country to sit in a seminar. They have work to do and assume they'll just get farther behind for no purpose. Our goal was to create an environment that would replace this natural reluctance with excitement. They realize their day in our RESULTS Center is indicative of their company's commitment to them and to innovation and openness.

We've shared these pretty minute details about our RESULTS Center to inspire you to search for ways to enhance your company's *Vibe* with innovative distinctions in your workspace and in the ways you serve your customers. In the next chapter, we'll talk more about infusing innovation into your environment so people will clamor to work for you and to do business with you.

Chapter 1
VIPs

For the Individual:

1. Openness is a quality that adds *Vibe* to your personal leadership brand.
2. A component of openness is curiosity. You enhance your brand's *Vibe* by showing you're open to growing and learning.
3. Seeking advice from mentors who have been successful in areas where you want to grow is another way to prove you're receptive to learning and growing.

For Your Organization:

4. Whether you're a CEO or other top executive or you lead a department, you want to be constantly seeking out expertise to bring innovative ideas and solutions to the business plan you're following. If you don't have fresh ideas flowing in, you could be stuck in outdated practices that will cause you to lose your relevancy as well as your positive *Vibe*.
5. You can often experience a company's *Vibe* by the innovative way it designs its workspace and serves its customers.
6. You can make every aspect of your space so intentional that people are already captivated with your energy before you even walk into the room.

CHAPTER 2 WARDROBE/ ENVIRONMENT

For the Individual Leader: Wardrobe

You have seven seconds to make a first impression, and everything about you must be finely tuned because the *Vibe* you give off at that moment is the one people will remember about you.

Most of us have heard the expression "You eat with your eyes." This saying validates the fact that presentation goes a long way when meeting someone for the first time; and remember, today we often see people for the first time on a web call. How you present yourself tells other people quite a bit about you. If you take care of your hygiene, future business partners or employers are likely going to think more highly of your work ethic. If you take care of yourself, you're probably going to put much more effort into your work. Nothing demands or demonstrates excellence quite like how you dress.

When you have the right wardrobe and everything about you looks great, others talk positively about you and respect you even before they meet you. That's important because, like it or not, people judge first with their eyes.

YOU HAVE SEVEN SECONDS TO MAKE A FIRST IMPRESSION, AND EVERYTHING ABOUT YOU MUST BE FINELY TUNED BECAUSE THE VIBE YOU GIVE OFF AT THAT MOMENT IS THE ONE PEOPLE WILL REMEMBER ABOUT YOU.

Remember the executive I called to come to the RESULTS Center to meet the founders of a company who were looking for a CEO? Several months before, I had sent him to a good friend to help him tune up his wardrobe and appearance to give off the best possible *Vibe*. He showed up looking just like I hoped he would—like a million-dollar CEO with extraordinary *Vibe*. His grooming and wardrobe gave the appearance of a sharp corporate executive. He wasn't wearing a three-piece suit. He was dressed in a nice shirt that was appropriate for the type of business the founders were creating, with a nice jacket and pants that matched. His appearance and actions were exactly what he needed to make the best possible impression, and I could see it take effect in how fast he resonated with this group.

My friend Evan York is a famous wardrobe consultant, and he and I have strategically discussed the fact that your clothing not only reflects your self-image; it also reflects how you live your life. The ideal picture you want to convey, of course, is that you conduct your life with fine detail and deliberate attention. For example, a tie that ties well and looks perfect and shoes that are shined and are appropriate for your well-coordinated outfit give the appearance that your life is well kept and organized.

YOUR CLOTHING NOT ONLY REFLECTS YOUR SELF-IMAGE; IT ALSO REFLECTS HOW YOU LIVE YOUR LIFE. THE IDEAL PICTURE YOU WANT TO CONVEY, OF COURSE, IS THAT YOU CONDUCT YOUR LIFE WITH FINE DETAIL AND DELIBERATE ATTENTION.

My wife and I just moved into our new condo one minute from the RESULTS Center, and I invested about twenty hours just designing our closet. In my line of work, I'm meeting people in person or on screen or standing before groups almost every day. What most people don't know is that I intentionally and strategically dress for whomever I'm seeing or meeting with each day. I want to have easy access to my choices because my wardrobe has been strategically acquired, tailormade, and carefully pruned. There's no junk in my closet to suck my energy—in fact, just the opposite! Everything about my wardrobe is purposefully chosen to present the kind of *Vibe* I want people to see, experience, and remember.

Daniel's family business is all about creating jewelry and custom belt buckles. For my birthday last year, he went out of his way to have a special belt buckle made for me with our clarity, focus, and execution logo in it, made of three different colors of metal. It's a cool buckle, and just wearing it actually gives me *Vibe*. Clothes can often do that.

Modeling the look of others is a great way to determine your style. Find someone who inspires you and gives the impression you want to give and model your clothing after that person. You can also glean ideas from magazines, websites, and blogs to constantly sharpen your image.

I had a big *aha* a few years ago when I was talking to my great friend Tammy Kling about my wardrobe. At the time I had a picture of Sean Connery on my vision board because I wanted to model my wardrobe after him so I could grow older stylishly. Tammy said, "No, you have a flaw on your *Belief Window*." She said, "You don't want to wear old stylish clothes; you want to wear young stylish clothes." That was an epiphany for me (Google my Impact Model blog on *aha*'s). I was unconsciously moving into the demographic of looking older versus projecting the look of a younger, vibrant person with energy! I immediately cleaned out my closet and gave away thousands of dollars' worth of Robert Graham and Tommy Bahama shirts. Now I buy different brands, I tailor my clothes even more, and I cut my hair differently (and often—every ten days).

As Daniel was growing up, his family enjoyed wearing Cartier jewelry, and they ended up buying and running one of the oldest custom jewelry companies in the Dallas area, which custom makes both men's and ladies' accessories. (Check their business out at Bohlinmade.com.) They understand that having the right accessories that complement your wardrobe contributes to the impression you make. You want to walk in with the right cufflinks, belt buckle, jewelry, purse, tie, shoes, or any other accessories that will make the best impact on your brand's *Vibe*. (Just wearing a watch or handbag can give you *Vibe*.) When you have great accessories, you stand apart from others, and you often make an energetic connection with them.

A former business partner said to us, "Attention is currency," and he was right. When people notice you, they remember your brand and the *Vibe* they get from it. He told us a story about a guy who went to a business meeting in a foreign country wearing gold tennis shoes. The king of the country called him on the carpet for it, and he responded by saying, "How many people have you met, and how many do you remember? You'll always remember the guy with the gold tennis shoes." The king said, "You're right." His accessories may have been a bit unorthodox, and yet they were the key to getting the king's attention.

ATTENTION IS CURRENCY. WHEN PEOPLE NOTICE YOU, THEY REMEMBER YOUR BRAND AND THE VIBE THEY GET FROM IT.

If you wear a beard, it's just as important to keep it properly trimmed as it is to wear the right clothes and have the right accessories. Remember, in the eyes of others, your appearance is aligned with what you do, and you want to portray a professional who is well kept and organized. An unkempt beard screams just the opposite.

I wanted to help Daniel enhance his *Vibe*, so I bought him a red Ferrari for Christmas. That would boost anyone's *Vibe*, right? Well, Daniel can't exactly drive this Ferrari; it's a red beard trimmer and clipper with a Ferrari motor in it. Daniel had mentioned that his girlfriend loves his beard, so I thought, *Okay, I want to practice what I preach in* Strategic Gifting [a book I coauthored last year], *so I should get something that's important to his inner circle.* Actually, I had bought one for myself a few weeks before and had been enjoying it, and I knew it would be the perfect Christmas gift for Daniel.

I believe it was Barbara Corcoran from *Shark Tank* who said, "Your wardrobe is your secret weapon—not just because of how you come across, but also how it makes you feel. It's almost like your special armor." Of course, that also applies to your overall look, including grooming and accessories. Make it all work for you to create a powerful *Vibe*.

For the Organization: Environment
Energy matters. As we've said, when people are considering working for or doing business with you, their decision often hinges—consciously or subconsciously—on your company's *Vibe*. And the *Vibe* emanating from your organization's environment carries a loud voice in their decision.

Energy matters. When people are considering working for or doing business with you, their decision often hinges—consciously or subconsciously—on your company's Vibe. And the Vibe emanating from your organization's environment carries a loud voice in their decision.

Your organization's *Vibe* actually starts with anything visual: your email signature, your website, your first Zoom call, or even in the parking lot. Do you want to work for a company whose parking lot is filled with trash and broken bottles? Is your website user-friendly and easy to navigate? Do your parking and directional signs remove guesswork and frustration from your visitors' first impression? Do they say where to go or where to park and how to get into your building or office? When visitors come in, who welcomes them and how are they greeted? When you enter a company's offices and you are greeted with a bell to summon whoever hears it, what is your reaction? All this may seem standard to some, yet it's overlooked by many. Unfortunately, many even see it as a prime area for cost cutting. Yes, it is hard to trace the return on investment for these items, but consider the message sent to prospective clients and employees. You can often truly enhance your organization's *Vibe* by being innovative in the way you design your visitors' initial impression.

Is your company innovative in the way it operates? How about the design of your space? We've recently started partnering and working with Envision Dallas (formerly Dallas Lighthouse for the Blind [see www.envisionus.com]), which is one of the country's largest employers of people with visual impairments. Their workplace is a showcase of ingenious innovations. For example, they've installed audio in the foyer that can be programmed to deliver different greetings, such as

"Welcome to Envision." And when someone walks up the stairs, a bell rings to alert the vision-impaired employees that someone is coming up. When Daniel and I went there to meet with their CEO, we were impressed with their open and innovative *Vibe*.

Another remarkably innovative company we've visited recently is Vari (formerly Varidesk). Because they make such cool desks, we had some interest in their company before we went to meet with Jeff Lamb, their CEO; once we toured their place we were captivated. We were blown away by so many of their innovations, such as their wall branding, the layout of their space, and the thought behind the convergent spaces for eating. They took a best practice from Google, which was putting the healthy food and drinks in the front of their food bins and frosting the glass over the sodas and unhealthy food in the back. These foods are available; they just aren't visible. All these components together create an amazing space. It's the type of environment that would likely make a forward-looking person think, *I can see myself working here. This is in alignment with my personal vision.* If that's your company's environment and you're wanting to influence a prospective customer or employee, your sale is probably already made because your brand's *Vibe* did all the work for you.

Several years ago, I invested in a company called Dogtopia, the nation's fastest-growing dog daycare, boarding, and spa franchise.

Last year Dogtopia ranked as the number one pet services franchise in *Entrepreneur* Magazine's 41st Annual Franchise 500® List. It's performing so well because of the extraordinary *Vibe* we've been able to create that attracts "doggie parents" by the droves. If you want to experience the company's *Vibe*, check out the website at Dogtopia.com or visit one of our centers.

We encourage you to be intentional with each space within your workplace. If it's a workroom, consider what would make it the best, most focus-centric workroom. If it's a break room or lunch room, what components (such as lighting) could you add to it to cultivate a culture behind it? An inside room with a vending machine, coffee machine, and some tables with terrible lighting is completely demoralizing. If it's a space for inspiration, what can you put in the room that will stimulate inspiration (*e.g.*, words, phrases, or photos)? Whatever asset you want to have, make it exceptional from the best practices you've experienced.

BE INTENTIONAL WITH EACH SPACE WITHIN YOUR WORKPLACE. WHATEVER ASSET YOU WANT TO HAVE, MAKE IT EXCEPTIONAL FROM THE BEST PRACTICES YOU'VE EXPERIENCED.

Constantly search the environments you're in for energy you can bring into your space. By being open, you can actively gain ideas and best practices everywhere you go, taking in what you like and building that into your culture and environment and making it a part of your *Vibe*. For example, we constantly look at Apple and other design-oriented companies that have paid big money for designers to help them create a *Vibe*. There is nothing wrong with copying from the best who can afford the cutting edge.

> Constantly be searching the environments you're in for energy you can bring into your space. By remaining open, you can actively gain ideas and best practices everywhere you go, taking in what you like and building that into your culture and environment.

Don't get stuck in thinking you need to compare office to office. Whatever *Vibe* you want your organization to have, make sure it has a familiar design and a conducive aspect to it. If you go into a tavern and like what they've done, bring it into your office environment. If you go into an American Express lounge or a Centurion Black Card lounge, you'll see that there's a very intentional setup in these places that creates a certain *Vibe*; and if you like it, you can model their decor. You don't have to just compare apples to apples. The important thing is that you create a *Vibe* that conveys your company's energy.

Here at the RESULTS Center, we look after our employees' physical *Vibe* and their mental *Vibe* as well. We do not want our employees or our clients to be overwhelmed. Having opportunities to recharge during breaks can be the difference between failure or success. And remember, the little things must not be overlooked. We understand that for people to perform at the best of their ability, we must take care of what can eat away at their psyche, no matter how big or small. Psyche management must not go unnoticed within a company.

We encourage custom mats, wall lettering, and even historical showcasing.

CHAPTER 2
VIPs

For the Individual:

1. You have seven seconds to make a first impression, and everything about you must be finely tuned because the *Vibe* you give off at that moment is the one people will remember about you.
2. Your clothing not only reflects your self-image; it also reflects how you live your life. The ideal picture you want to convey, of course, is that you conduct your life with fine detail and deliberate attention.
3. Attention is currency. When people notice you, they remember your brand and the *Vibe* they get from it.

For the Organization:

4. Energy matters. When people are considering working for or doing business with you, their decision often hinges—consciously or subconsciously—on your company's *Vibe*. And the *Vibe* emanating from your organization's environment carries a loud voice in their decision.
5. Be intentional with each space within your workplace. Make every element of your physical plant an asset, and make it exceptional by gleaning from the best practices you've experienced.
6. Constantly be searching the environments you're around for energy you can bring into your space. By remaining open, you can actively gain ideas and best practices everywhere you go, taking in what you like and building that into your culture and environment.

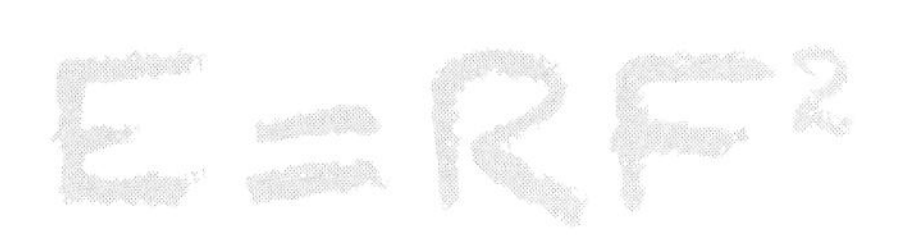

CHAPTER 3
LINKEDIN OR WIKI/ WEBSITE AND REVIEWS

For the Individual: LinkedIn

Every day we get more virtual about everything. Do you agree? When people are considering doing business with you or working for you or with your organization, often the first thing they do is . . . you got it—go online and start clicking. They look up the history, the leadership, and everything else about your organization. So their first introduction to your *Vibe*—or lack thereof—often starts with their research of all your electronic channels.

When you have met someone at a mixer whom you were interested in following up with, you instinctively go to their LinkedIn page. If they don't have one, that's it. They don't exist. If they do, you'll likely examine it with a fine-tooth comb before you send them that message. Chances are, you will also visit their company's Web page. If it looks like something from the 1990s, you will almost certainly assume they work for a backward company. Those two pages are your introduction to their world.

> The first introduction people have to your *Vibe*—or lack thereof—often starts with their research of all your electronic channels. The goal is to maintain motivation, positive energy, and even spirit throughout your digital presence.

The goal is to maintain motivation and positive energy throughout your digital presence. The good news is, it's easy to manage your *Vibe* electronically, even though it does take thought and effort. For example, when people click on your LinkedIn profile, the pictures you use, your profile presentation, your endorsements, and the videos you link to can all express your *Vibe.*

WITH MUCH THOUGHT AND EFFORT, YOU CAN EASILY MANAGE YOUR *VIBE* ELECTRONICALLY.

LinkedIn (today) is one of the most popular tools for researching people and businesses, and it's an excellent platform for making connections and establishing your *Vibe.* People look at everything. They want to know your history; they are interested in who you know and are curious about what you've accomplished; and they even want to see who recommends you and who has endorsed you, and specifically what they have said about you. They want to see if you have strong recommendations from respected leaders in your industry. Your LinkedIn profile can actually help you build trust with prospective clients or employees, as they can see evidence of where you have added value. Consequently, it's extremely important to keep your profile information and your endorsements and recommendations updated.

YOUR LINKEDIN PROFILE CAN ACTUALLY HELP YOU BUILD TRUST WITH PROSPECTIVE CLIENTS OR EMPLOYEES, AS THEY CAN SEE EVIDENCE OF WHERE YOU HAVE ADDED VALUE.

Study my LinkedIn account—Tony Jeary, The RESULTS Guy™— to see the *energy* it projects from the very beginning. The first thing you see is this handpicked picture, which shows me speaking on stage to a huge crowd of people, with an insert that shows me autographing a book (which implies my experience level as an authority). Both pictures were carefully chosen.

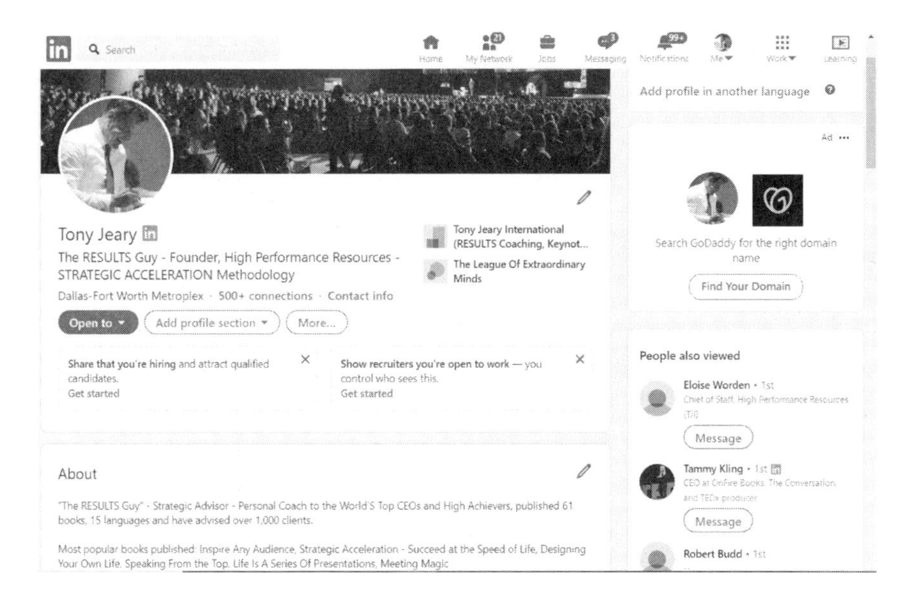

As you scroll down, you can "feel" what most say is excitement and energy through:

- The power-packed profile
- Hundreds of endorsements from top clients all over the globe (I've invested hours and hours obtaining these endorsements, which is something you might consider.)
- Recommendations from many industry leaders (Again, making the effort to request these might be worth it for you, too.)
- A picture of me interacting with a participant
- One of my quotes, "The enemy of mastery is often greatness" (Ask me about this sometime.)
- A carefully thought-out video that targets the people I want for clients: high achievers who want to win more

If you have a high-enough profile, you may be listed in Wikipedia, which would appear in online search results. In fact, an entry in Wikipedia is among the most powerful credentials you can have. If you have a Wiki page, it is extremely important to maintain its accuracy and keep it up to date and projecting as much *Vibe* as possible in an online encyclopedia that is open to edit by anyone and everyone.

For Your Organization: Website

Just as is true with an individual, often the first introduction to your organization's *Vibe* will be through your website, as that's typically the first source people access when they're checking out your organization's brand.

> Often the first introduction to your organization's *Vibe* will be through your website, as that's typically the first source people access when they're checking out your organization's brand.

Again, it's easier to show than tell (and often more powerful). So let's take a look at one of my thirteen websites, tonyjeary.com. Here's one of the three scrolling pictures on the home page:

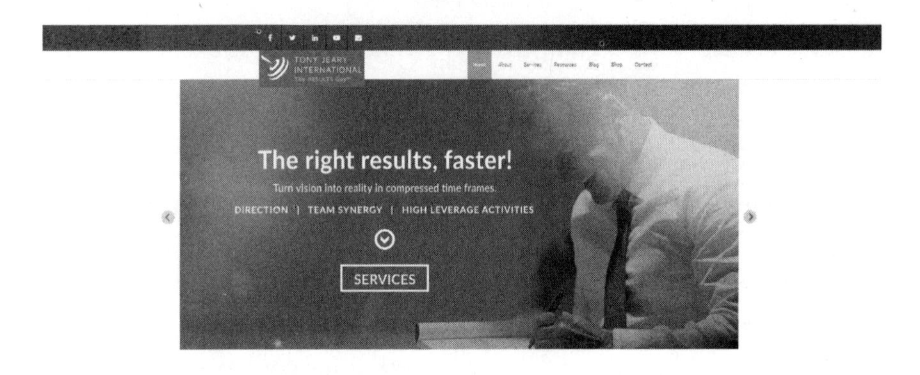

Remember, a picture is worth a thousand words. Choose your pictures wisely. We believe this picture exudes success, excitement, and *Vibe* with:

- Its blue color
- My bullseye logo, company name, and moniker (The RESULTS Guy™) in the red box
- My picture (again, autographing a book)
- Two of my taglines:
  - The right results, faster!
  - Turn vision into reality in compressed timeframes.

(Are your websites and pictures full of *Vibe*? Do you have taglines that are current, interesting, and inspiring?)

- Three of our high-demand offerings:
  - Direction
  - Team synergy
  - High Leverage Activities

A PICTURE IS WORTH A THOUSAND WORDS. CHOOSE YOUR PICTURES FOR YOUR WEBSITE WISELY, SO THEY EXUDE SUCCESS, EXCITEMENT, AND *VIBE*.

Check out the energy in this paragraph from my "About: Tony Jeary" page: "In just a few hours with Tony Jeary and his team, you can forever change the way you think, operate, and perform. We truly enjoy helping successful clients reach the next level, and we often take them all the way to the mastery level. If you want proof, check out our track record."

Brainstorm with your team (including your marketing colleagues) to see how you can leverage *Vibe* throughout your digital presence, and then see how it affects your results. I believe you'll be happy you did.

BRAINSTORM WITH YOUR TEAM (INCLUDING YOUR MARKETING COLLEAGUES) TO SEE HOW YOU CAN LEVERAGE *VIBE* THROUGHOUT YOUR DIGITAL PRESENCE.

In this chapter, we have covered the two most important sources for spotlighting you and your company, but what about other avenues? Be sure to research where your target audience exists; you will want to consider demographics like age, location, interests, and so forth. Take Pinterest, for instance. Though multiple generational brackets use this platform, the most active group consists of millennial mothers. If you are targeting teenagers, it's good to know that the largest demographic for Twitter includes ages under thirty. Knowing your audience and leveraging your *Vibe* accordingly will help you promote your business.

CHAPTER 3
VIPs

For the Individual: LinkedIn

1. The first introduction people have to your *Vibe*—or lack thereof—often starts with their research of all your electronic channels. The goal is to maintain motivation, positive energy, and even spirit throughout your digital presence.
2. With much thought and effort, you can easily manage your *Vibe* electronically.
3. Your LinkedIn profile can actually help you build trust with prospective clients or employees, as they can see evidence of where you have added value.

For the Organization: Website

4. Often the first introduction to your organization's *Vibe* will be through your website, as that's typically the first source people access when they're checking out your organization's brand.
5. A picture is worth a thousand words. Choose your pictures for your website wisely so they exude success, excitement, and *Vibe*.
6. Brainstorm with your team (including your marketing colleagues) to see how you can leverage *Vibe* throughout your digital presence.

CHAPTER 4 ACCOMPLISHMENTS/ CUSTOMER TESTIMONIALS

For the Individual: Accomplishments

This chapter complements the previous chapter because we're still talking about what people want to know about you as a leader. First, do you have a personal web page? And we aren't necessarily talking about a blog. We are talking about your own page with its own URL. No, it is not over the top self-centered. Thousands of writers, professionals, and executives have them, and you should consider one.

LinkedIn has a format that restricts what you say and how you say it. The same is true of Facebook. A personal page is all yours to do with as you please. If some variation of your name is available (*e.g.*, tony.jeary) grab it.

Your digital portfolio needs to include information about your accomplishments, such as:

- Have you published articles, blogs, books, or perhaps columns? (I write a column for *SUCCESS* magazine called "Ask The RESULTS Guy™.")
- Have you served on any panels?
- Are you part of or do you support a nonprofit organization through philanthropy (giving or serving)? (For example, I partner with and support Envision [envisionus.com], one of America's largest employers of the blind and visually impaired.)
- Are you serving on a board or have you served on one in the past?
- Do you publish videos, including on YouTube?
- Have you made any public speeches, or have you done a TED Talk?

All these can add to your persona or *Vibe* as a trusted leader in business or in your community. Today's world is different; people take a more holistic view and make judgments about your leadership based on what you've done and whether you're contributing to a better world.

> Your accomplishments can add to your persona or *Vibe* as a leader because people today take a more holistic view and make judgments about your leadership based on what you've done and whether you're contributing to a better world.

PEOPLE ALSO OFTEN LOOK FOR WHAT THEY CAN DISCERN ABOUT YOUR VIBE ON A MORE PERSONAL SIDE—BOTH ONLINE AND OFFLINE.

My personal office is designed to help create a *Vibe* and so should yours. Above my bookshelves visitors see in large capital letters the word *THINK*. That's because the main thing I've devoted my vocation to is helping others think. That's something I'm really grateful to be known for. And the letters on my wall also remind me to think when I walk into my office.

If you have bookshelves and walls, what you do with them is important. Anyone who sits in your office is going to study what you have on your shelves and what you have on your walls. It is just human curiosity. Your office should be personal and not a just a decorator's idea of what you should have. Your walls and shelves can and should tell your life's story and display your achievements in a way where you don't have to. It is actually far more subtle than telling people about your accomplishments.

All these things I believe contribute to my *Vibe* and the *Vibe* of our organization. I don't share all this with you to be arrogant. I just want to provide ideas to you from my own experience. My intentionality in this area is to help you communicate your accomplishments in a way that will give you credibility and let people see your *Vibe* as a leader. When they do, it often makes them want to work around you or beside you and/or be mentored by you. (As a side note, I've been able to attract very unique interns to work for us, which I attribute to our *Vibe.)*

WHEN PEOPLE SEE YOUR *VIBE* AS A LEADER, IT OFTEN MAKES THEM WANT TO WORK AROUND YOU OR BESIDE YOU AND/OR BE MENTORED BY YOU.

For the Organization: Customer Testimonials

What do your clients say about your company? There is nothing more important as a demonstration of what the people who paid you and invested hours with you thought about their experience than that they had good things to say about you and your organization. It is perfectly acceptable to have letters of commendation from clients, customers, employees, and team members, strategically placed around your office. It is great for organizational pride and for creating a *Vibe* that is more than a flatscreen deep.

Your website should be loaded with customer testimonials—as many as you have. At the risk of over-tooting my own horn, I do believe our set of company websites illustrates the point. If you visit tonyjeary.com website again, you'll notice that we have many client testimonials in the "About: Testimonials" section, and also on the "Services" pages. They all show credibility and *Vibe* to anyone viewing the website.

CUSTOMER TESTIMONIALS SHOW CREDIBILITY AND *VIBE* TO ANYONE VIEWING YOUR WEBSITE.

Take a look at another of our websites, StrategicAcceleration.com, which is the core resource site for my signature book, *Strategic Acceleration: Succeed at the Speed of Life*. This screenshot is from the home page:

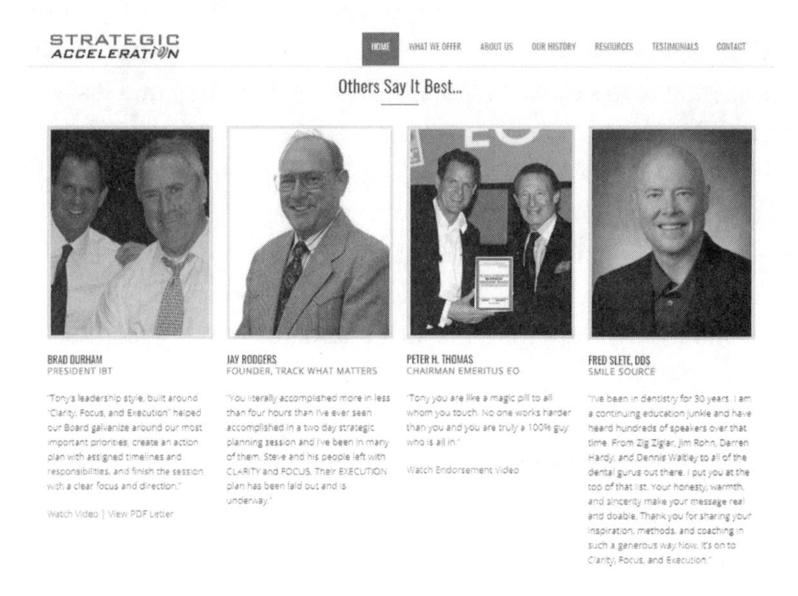

If you look carefully, you'll see where we've added links to videos and PDFs of letters to give credibility beyond just a simple quote.

Vibrant testimonials/reviews that include pictures, videos, and letters speak loudly because social proof is such a powerful tool today. Leverage them liberally on your website, in your publications, and, in fact, in most of your marketing tools. (See the PDF of a little book we published called *Impact*, which is loaded with stories, testimonials, and reference messages that supplement our organization's *Vibe*. Email *info@tonyjeary.com* and we'll share them with you.)

VIBRANT TESTIMONIALS/REVIEWS THAT INCLUDE PICTURES, VIDEOS, AND LETTERS SPEAK LOUDLY BECAUSE SOCIAL PROOF IS SUCH A POWERFUL TOOL TODAY.

CHAPTER 4 VIPs

For the Individual: Accomplishments

1. Your accomplishments can add to your persona or *Vibe* as a leader because people today take a more holistic view and make judgments about your leadership based on what you've done and whether you're contributing to a better world.
2. People also often look for what they can discern about your *Vibe* on a more personal side—both online and offline.
3. When people see your *Vibe* as a leader, it often makes them want to work around you or beside you and/or be mentored by you.

For the Organization: Customer Testimonials

4. Customer testimonials show credibility and *Vibe* to anyone viewing your website.
5. Vibrant testimonials/reviews that include pictures, videos, and letters speak loudly because social proof is such a powerful tool today.

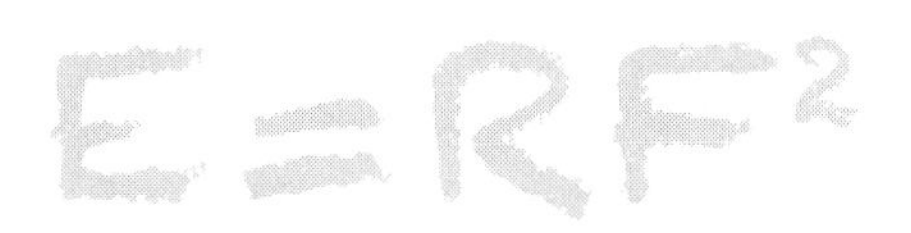

CHAPTER 5
ATTITUDE/CARING

For the Individual: Attitude

One of the chief characteristics people look for in a leader today is a caring attitude. Great leaders cultivate a healthy and positive culture that increases engagement and productivity and creates an atmosphere of cooperation. As the American poet Maya Angelou said, "People will forget what you said, people will forget what you did, but people will never forget how you made them feel." Leaders who truly care about their people get to know them well so they can discover what's important to them and how they can help them be their very best. A caring servant leader enhances an organization's *Vibe.*

GREAT LEADERS CULTIVATE A HEALTHY AND POSITIVE CULTURE THAT INCREASES ENGAGEMENT AND PRODUCTIVITY AND CREATES AN ATMOSPHERE OF COOPERATION.

Daniel is such a leader. As the GM for TJI, several weeks ago he received a gift box from several of our team members who wanted to show their appreciation.

A CARING SERVANT LEADER ENHANCES AN ORGANIZATION'S *VIBE*.

Here's an example of Daniel's caring leadership style: we had an important project recently with an extremely tight deadline that required extraordinary effort on the part of all team members. Daniel not only made key contributions to the effort himself; he provided support for other team members to the tune of working all night several nights. He has brought positivity, fun, and a spirit of cooperation to new levels in our office. One of the new practices we've instituted under Daniel's leadership is allowing team members to leave at 4:00 p.m., unless there's a rush project that needs to be completed. These and other selfless efforts prove him to be a servant leader who brings a great deal of *Vibe* to our organization.

Great leaders understand that a company is only as strong as its weakest link. It is vital that you let your employees know they are not just another number within the company, but that you care about them and acknowledge them as a member of your team. This does not mean you need to invite them to your next family Thanksgiving dinner, but it does mean you need to go out of your way to let them know their opinions are valued. There should be a *Vibe* of constant recognition. Even a simple "Hi" or "Nice job yesterday" tells the employees you know they exist and are glad they are part of your team. Just this simple form of recognition will make them want to work harder for you. One of the best catalysts for growth is having a caring culture where employees know they are contributing to the company.

Face it, your employees/team members are customer facing. They are an extension of your *Vibe*. If your people are motivated to deliver more than promised and take pride in their accomplishments, your office and ecosystem will hum to your *Vibe*.

NOTHING CRUSHES CULTURE FASTER THAN TYRANNY.

Your culture is perhaps your organization's most fragile asset. Anytime you subtract someone from the organization, you run the risk of losing a little of that *High-Performing Team* synergy (*see* chapter 8). Other team members may fear they are next, which could negatively affect productivity and open an environment for conflict. People need to know they are important and striving toward a common goal in order to bring the company success.

We recently ran across this "Balance Sheet of Life" on the internet. Though it would be a great fit in several chapters of this book, it lends itself well to the concept of creating *Vibe* by having a caring attitude. Although the original source is unknown, it is a very popular item on social media. Perhaps that's because many people are taking stock of their lives.

BALANCE SHEET OF LIFE

The most destructive habit ....Worry
The greatest joy .... Giving
The greatest loss .... Loss of Self-respect
The most satisfying work .... Helping Others
The ugliest personality trait .... Selfishness
The greatest "shot in the arm" .... Encouragement
The greatest problem to overcome .... Fear
The most effective sleeping pill .... Peace of Mind
The most crippling failure disease .... Excuses
The most powerful force in life .... Love
The most dangerous act .... A Gossip
The world's most incredible computer ..... The Brain
The worst thing to be without .... Hope
The deadliest weapon .... The Tongue
The two most power-filled words .... "I Can"
The greatest asset .... Faith
The most worthless emotion .... Selp-pity
The most beautiful attire .... Smile!
The most prized possession .... Integrity
The most powerful channel of communication .. Prayer
The most contagious spirit .... Enthusiasm

LIFE ends, when you stop DREAMING. HOPE ends, when you stop BELIEVING. LOVE ends, when you stop CARING. So, please share this BALANCE SHEET OF LIFE. FRIENDSHIP ends when you stop SHARING.

For the Organization: Caring

Similarly, an organization whose brand includes the integral component of caring is one whose leadership understands and cares for the values and situations of others. Caring is demonstrated every day in both big and little things, which causes a company to have *Vibe*.

AN ORGANIZATION WHOSE BRAND INCLUDES THE INTEGRAL COMPONENT OF CARING IS ONE WHOSE LEADERSHIP UNDERSTANDS AND CARES FOR THE VALUES AND SITUATIONS OF OTHERS. SUCH A COMPANY HAS *VIBE*.

For example, does your organization offer flexibility in supporting a person's personal schedule? Sharon, our controller, enjoys having the flexibility to spend time with her granddaughter. Or maybe it's a small matter like respecting your individual team member's opinions about wearing a mask during the coronavirus pandemic.

Or perhaps it's supporting your team members in understanding what their goals are. For years, we've had a goals board in our office where we post both organizational and individual goals. We're very mindful of what our team members want to accomplish, and we offer encouragement and support to help them achieve their goals.

A team member who worked for us several years ago was one of the most exemplary as far as saying, "Just tell me what you want accomplished." I took the time to understand what was important to her, and one of her goals was to see the world. As our session manager, she traveled with me to meet with different client organizations, and she ended up going to a hundred cities during her six-year tenure. She also wanted to pay off her school loans, so I helped her make additional money through our bonus plan. When she left the company, she had no debt and far more savings than most her age. She had also amassed contacts, a huge asset for a young person moving forward in a career. She is an incredibly special woman and added tons to our Vibe over the years. She got the concept of Vibe, and she was an extension of it for us.

Here are other ways you can show caring to your team:

- Offer personal and professional development opportunities
- Provide and celebrate meaningful work opportunities
- Share meaningful results with people
- Develop shared values, purpose, mission, and vision
- Conduct onboarding and exit interviews with an emphasis on retention

- Provide for promotion from within and help with clear career paths
- Provide for autonomy at their workstation or office
- Provide for the physical, mental, and social comfort
- Develop mentor opportunities
- Develop award and recognition opportunities[1]

Not every organization can offer individual perk and over-the-top attention. Yet experience with hundreds of organizations over the decades has shown clearly that investing in people is the best investment you can make. This type of philosophy begins at the top, and it's that exemplary type of caring that brings *Vibe* to your organization.

Help your team members win to the extent you can, as their winning results in your winning as an organization. This type of philosophy begins at the top, and it's that exemplary type of caring that brings *Vibe* to your organization.

At Tony Jeary International, a successful *Strategic Appreciation* model has been crafted to obtain optimum employee retention. This model is made up of these three categories: (1) compensation, (2) credit, and (3) culture. Grab their attention with the money we pay them, keep them with words of affirmation (give them credit), and develop a magnetic culture for future hires.

You need all three concepts for this model to succeed. The structure will crumble if reliant on just one of the above areas. For instance, if you only focus on compensation, employees may be happy with their pay no matter whether they work in a productive environment. However, in the event of an economic crisis when you would be forced to cut back on their paychecks, you have no assurance your employees would remain faithful to the company and stay. If you have a good grasp on credit and culture as well as compensation, you can be more confident that the environment would maintain employee happiness even in times of constriction. If you emphasize quality of life by using the *Strategic Appreciation* model, you can rest more assured about the stability of your company.

CHAPTER 5
VIPS

For the Individual Leader: Attitude

1. Great leaders cultivate a healthy and positive culture that increases engagement and productivity and creates an atmosphere of cooperation.
2. A caring servant leader enhances an organization's *Vibe.*

For the Organization: Caring

3. An organization whose brand includes the integral component of caring is one whose leadership understands and cares for the values and situations of others. Such a company has *Vibe.*
4. Help your team members win to the extent you can, as their winning results in your winning as an organization. This type of philosophy begins at the top, and it's that exemplary type of caring that brings *Vibe* to your organization.

PART 2
LEADERSHIP

Outstanding leaders go out of their way to boost the self-esteem of their personnel. If people believe in themselves, it's amazing what they can accomplish.
—Sam Walton

What is a leader? Here's my definition: A leader is one who sets a clear vision and shares that vision with others in a way that compels them to willingly focus their efforts to ensure the successful execution of the vision.

Leadership can apply either to an individual or to a team of individuals running an organization. Often organizations are compared based on their leadership teams. The best leadership teams raise their organization to the top and become known as leaders in their particular industry or genre.

For example, Apple carries the leadership role in the cell phone space. That's not to say that many of the others aren't great; it's just that Apple has taken that lead position because of their extraordinary leadership team. Their doing so gives them a few extra points of *Vibe*.

As an individual, you may be asking, *How do people look at me as a leader? Do I cast the vision for our organization? Do I have a level of self-discipline that people admire? Do they look up to me as a strong, energized leader they want to work for? Do I really work at fostering team comradery? Do I exude confidence, enthusiasm, and self-assurance?*

If you're a member of an organization's leadership team, you may be asking these questions: *Is our organization a leader in our niche/industry? If not, how can we strengthen our leadership team to get us there? Does our leadership team exude* Vibe, *which draws people to want to work here?*

In this section, we're going to unpack how you can create more *Vibe*, both as an individual leader and as a member of an organization's leadership team.

CHAPTER 6 GOALS/MISSION, VISION, STRATEGIC OBJECTIVES

For the Individual: Goals

Whether you're an individual who leads a department or an entire organization, or you're an entrepreneur who runs a company or who is in a network marketing space, many people look up to you. We believe if you're modeling solid goalsetting behaviors, you're a leader who is adding to your *Vibe.*

IF YOU'RE MODELING GREAT GOALSETTING BEHAVIORS, YOU'RE A LEADER WHO IS ADDING TO YOUR *VIBE.*

As a goal-oriented leader, it's useful to be aware of your reticular activating system (RAS), a set of nerves at the bottom of the brain that allows you to bring things into your brain that you need, want, or desire. Case in point: when you buy a new car, you often suddenly start seeing those same cars all around you, as if they suddenly materialized and had not been there all along. (You didn't notice them as much two weeks before.) You see, when you set a goal, your brain recognizes that's something you're interested in, and it starts allowing in pertinent thoughts and ideas it had previously ignored. The more you focus on your goals, the more information your brain allows in. That's why it's important to look at your goals often and keep them in front of you on a vision board.

Leaders with *Vibe* have a presence about them that is evidenced by the way they carry themselves and the atmosphere they bring with them, which stems from truly believing in themselves. Much of their confidence comes from identifying their core values, which affirm who they are and what they stand for, and which serve as the foundation for all their goals.

Recently I did an interview for an organization called Global Leaders Organization (GLO), which is partnered with Microsoft, and we piped it out across the country. People who watched the interview could feel my *Vibe*. Twenty minutes after the interview, the Microsoft executives who had watched it live said, "This guy has energy! We want to have him do this same interview for us, and we want to pipe it to everyone who is on LinkedIn." *Vibe* matters. I have been friends with Michelle, my host and GLO's founder, for decades. She has tons of *Vibe* herself, and with our working together, energy was flowing and the event went very well. Both of us wanted to pour *Vibe* into our viewers' lives.

> Leaders with *Vibe* have a presence about them that is evidenced by the way they carry themselves and the atmosphere they bring with them, which stems from truly believing in themselves. Much of their confidence comes from identifying their core values, which affirm who they are and what they stand for, and which serve as the foundation for all their goals.

Many people from across the country were judging our *Vibe* in this interview. And the subset of that was, they were wondering what kind of leader I am. Knowing my credentials, they wondered if they were going to absorb information about me as a coach, as an advisor, and as a person who strategically helps organizations grow. In essence, they were wondering what my motivations and goals are. The more you can articulate where you're going and what you do, the more it adds to your leadership *Vibe*. People want to see if you can add leadership *Vibe* to their world as an employee, team member, or even a partner.

I've been setting goals since the age of seventeen years old. I now have over 100 pages of goals. Too much of a good thing? For some, undoubtedly, but I have found setting large numbers of goals is how I can stay focused. You may be thinking, *Well, that applies to you; does it apply*

THE MORE YOU CAN ARTICULATE WHERE YOU'RE GOING AND WHAT YOU DO, THE MORE IT ADDS TO YOUR LEADERSHIP *VIBE*. PEOPLE WANT TO SEE IF YOU CAN ADD LEADERSHIP *VIBE* TO THEIR WORLD AS AN EMPLOYEE, TEAM MEMBER, OR EVEN A PARTNER.

to me? Yes! Everyone you touch as a leader makes a judgment, and the more you can articulate with clarity what you're about, the more it adds to your *Vibe* and the more attractive you are as a leader.

For the Organization: Mission, Vision, and Strategic Objectives

As the leader of our organization, I'm very clear on our vision and mission, and I want everyone who works for me to be clear. You should want that as well.

This is a page copied from my business goals file:

Business Framework

Vision: *CLARITY of where are we going*

Peter Drucker type demand. Positively impact our clients results in compressed time frames our competitors can't match whereby our global demand consistently exceeds our supply

Mission: *Why we exist*

Drive extraordinary results for clients and in return provide exceptional compensation that supports positive quality of life for each contributing TJI team member

HLAs: *Activities to FOCUS on*

1. ATTRACTING strong qualified business such as networking, speaking and sharing.
2. DELIVERING great value to our clients such as coaching, speaking and strategic facilitation engagement
3. CLARIFYING direction and improving operations
4. WISDOM ARSENAL continually build our processes, documented business acumen, and best practices and tools of all kind
5. ROLODEX nourish and build connections, extending value and positively communicating to and with them through email, resources, books and connections and other items of value

Values/Standards: *How we conduct ourselves and what we believe*

Our Motto: Give value, Do More Than is Expected...make every person, place or thing you're a part of better.

1. Save Tony's Time keeping him in front and serving our clients
2. KAIZEN means constant improvement for all team members... ongoing COEs, personal SWOTs and MOLO refinements
3. Keep all clean and ORGANIZED ...adds to our brand and makes us always ready
4. Constant LISTMAKING ... ensures prioritizing, accountability and execution of faster results (including CSFs)
5. Over-COMMUNICATE and calculate... helps ensure efforts are maximized. Avoid absolutes – words like never, always, can't – because all things are possible.
6. FOCUSed efforts on new flow of business/revenue. Daily priorities include pipeline management, SOW development and processing receivables. Remember cash is king!
7. Do (FIA) favors in advance – sharing, giving and helping others win.
8. Do THINGS NOW! Operate with a mindset of quick action and speed to completion while using "Production Before Perfection" – manage procrastination.
9. PROACTIVE everything (think ahead, prep ahead, do ahead, invoice ahead, deliver ahead and exceed expectations all around – internally and externally)
10. TEAM approach – overlap, cross-court, encourage, leverage each others' expertise, and together keep all eyes on getting things done, completed RESULTS produced hourly, daily and weekly.

Objectives: *What we want to accomplishMonthly*

1. Gross: $_____
2. Net: $_____
3. Receive 40 great referrals
4. Deliver: 16 calendar dates a month consisting of studio sessions, coaching, keynote experiences and Inner Circle Mastermind.
5. Visit 1 cool city
6. Expand IP (complete 2 new books, 7 new passports)
7. Grow Inner Circle participants

Strategies: *How we will compete*

Funnel approach using...

1. Work/Nourish Rolodex/Current clients repeating
2. Free autographed books
3. Web presence
4. PR
5. Campaigns & Promotions
6. Advertising
7. Speaking/Emceeing
8. Promoters
9. Super Promoters
10. New Contacts
11. Monthly List Blasts
12. Other

Actions/Tactics: *What needs EXECUTION*

1. Ongoing smart marketing
2. Sharing constant value on our clients
3. Growing our connections
4. Filling Tony's calendar with 4 types of high-yield activities: Strategic Facilitation, Results Coaching, Interactive Keynote Experiences, Web Trainings and Inner Circle Mastermind Events

CSFs (Critical Success Factors) or KPIs:

How we measure our success

1. Net revenue
2. Gross revenue
3. *Lessons From the Studio* subscription count
4. Earned income per month
5. Lead flow per week
6. Business booked in advance
7. Testimonials from clients (10+ a month)
8. Investments – gain and loss
9. Database details

As you can see, the vision of our organization is to create Peter Drucker-type demand, where we are positively impacting our clients' results in compressed timeframes that our competitors can't match. Our mission is to drive extraordinary results for our clients, and in return provide exceptional compensation that positively supports the life of each of our TJI team members.

Our vision and mission are not just about the customer, nor are they just about the ownership. They're about the customer, the ownership, and the people. If you want your organization to have *Vibe*, you'll want to bring value to all three subsets.

IF YOU WANT YOUR ORGANIZATION TO HAVE *VIBE*, YOU'LL WANT TO BRING VALUE TO THE CUSTOMER, THE OWNERSHIP, AND THE PEOPLE.

Every day when we walk in the front door of our RESULTS Center, we see our mantra on the wall in the foyer: "Give value; do more than expected." That's basically a short version of both our vision and our mission. And one way we create *Vibe* in our organization is to have it right out front where everyone who comes in can see what our mission is: to give value by doing more than expected.

One way your organizational leadership exhibits *Vibe* is by having your vision and mission statements posted—on your website as well as on your walls. It's important to convey them to people inside and outside of your organization and to make them part of your taglines.

ONE WAY YOUR ORGANIZATIONAL LEADERSHIP EXHIBITS *VIBE* IS BY HAVING YOUR VISION AND MISSION STATEMENTS POSTED—ON YOUR WEBSITE AS WELL AS ON YOUR WALLS.

When you are interviewing someone to work for your organization, the applicant makes a judgment about your leadership, based on how well you articulate the organization's mission and vision and your level of excitement as you share them. For example, if you show great enthusiasm about the founder of your company and his/her vision and belief in the quality of your products, that's a great win for both your *Vibe* and the company's.

As people associated with your organization—whether it's a strategic partner, a vendor, or anyone wanting to do business with your company—are getting to know your company, share with them your vision and mission. When people hear my passion as I'm describing what our organization is about—impacting people's thinking and thus their lives, and our goal of making every person, place, or thing we touch better—they can see my *Vibe* as a leader as well as the *Vibe* of our company.

> As people associated with your organization—whether it's a strategic partner, a vendor, or anyone wanting to do business with your company—are getting to know your company, share with them your vision and mission so they can see your *Vibe* as a leader as well as that of your company.

As a coach to the executives of American Airlines for years, I thought Doug Parker, the current president, did something very interesting when he took over. He asked all of us who consult for the company to participate in a quarterly webinar where we are briefed on the strategic objectives and priorities of American Airlines. Then, when we're coaching them or designing and building training resources for his workforce, we clearly know the company's mission, vision, and strategic objectives and can continue to do our work in alignment with them.

It is a brilliant strategy.

What are people saying about you? What kind of testimonials are on your website? Do you have a clear mission, vision, and objectives that people can get behind? All those things play into the level of *Vibe* your organization has.

CHAPTER 6
VIPs

For the Individual: Goals

1. If you're modeling great goalsetting behaviors, you're a leader who is adding to your *Vibe.*
2. Leaders with *Vibe* have a presence about them that is evidenced by the way they carry themselves and the atmosphere they bring with them, which stems from truly believing in themselves. Much of their confidence comes from identifying their core values, which affirm who they are and what they stand for, and which serve as the foundation for all their goals.
3. The more you can articulate where you're going and what you do, the more it adds to your leadership *Vibe.* People want to see if you can add leadership *Vibe* to their world as an employee, team member, or even a partner.

For the Organization: Mission, Vision, and Strategic Objectives

4. If you want your organization to have *Vibe*, you'll want to bring value to the customer, the ownership, and the people.
5. One way your organizational leadership exhibits *Vibe* is by having your vision and mission statements posted—on your website as well as on your walls.
6. As people associated with your organization—whether it's a strategic partner, a vendor, or anyone wanting to do business with your company—are getting to know your company, share with them your vision and mission so they can see your *Vibe* as a leader as well as that of your company.

CHAPTER 7 DISCIPLINE/ STANDARDS

For the Individual: Discipline

Leaders with *Vibe* know where they're going, and they stay on the path to get there. As a leader, you will have many people watching to see how well you follow your path.

LEADERS WITH *VIBE* KNOW WHERE THEY'RE GOING, AND THEY STAY ON THE PATH TO GET THERE.

Your discipline—or lack of it—plays out in many ways. Let's look at a few:

1. Showing up on time. I personally prefer for my team to not have to ever have to cover for me for being late. I want them to know I'm disciplined enough to be there—on time and prepared. When you're late, it creates a negative *Vibe*.

WHEN YOU'RE LATE, IT CREATES A NEGATIVE *VIBE*.

2. Achieving your goals. It's one thing to have goals; it's another thing to stay on the path to achieve them. Remember, people are watching.
3. Your health. Are you disciplined when it comes to your health? Do you support eating healthy and exercising? Like it or not, a thin waistline contributes to your *Vibe*.

LIKE IT OR NOT, A THIN WAISTLINE CONTRIBUTES TO YOUR *VIBE*.

4. Your attitude. Do you have a good attitude? Do you smile and appreciate others often?
5. Your mindset. Do you look for solutions rather than problems?
6. How organized you are. We'll talk more about this in Part 3, Organization.

Years ago, I was coaching the top three female executives at Walmart when there were about two million people working for the company. One day, one of the executives I was working with shared a problem. She had had a shot at being the number one female executive in all of Walmart, and they turned her down. When I asked why, she said, "Because my office was a mess. They said when they walked by and looked in my office, they didn't believe I had the organizational wherewithal to pull it off." She said, "You have to help me get my office cleaned up and coach me on this." A judgment was made on her lack of discipline, which was part of her *Vibe*, and it may have cost her hundreds of thousands—perhaps millions—of dollars over her career. She missed her promotion and ended up leaving Walmart, and it dramatically changed her life.

We're very aware of the effect cleanliness and order have on our *Vibe* as individuals and the *Vibe* of our agency. I'm looking out the window now and watching a great man who has been with us for fourteen years clean the windows at the RESULTS Center. We've asked him to clean our windows every other day because that's an extension of our *Vibe*. In fact, when people see our discipline in keeping our office space spotlessly clean, it validates our commitment to *Vibe*.

KEEPING THINGS CLEAN AND ORGANIZED VALIDATES YOUR *VIBE*.

When I walked in for the interview with GLO this week, I gave everyone in the whole place a copy of my book, *RESULTS Faster!* Before we started the interview, I was giving away dollar bills when people said something humorous (my signature "fun factor"). My goal in all of this was to get them saying, "Man, that guy brought some energy to our place today." My point is, I had the discipline to walk in with gifts and a set of books to give away. If I hadn't had that discipline, I wouldn't have brought as much energy.

We also had the discipline to be there early. When the lady who was going to interview me showed up, my team and I were standing out front in her parking lot. How many people show up for an interview early, ready to go, and bearing gifts?

For the Organization: Standards

Every organization should have clarity on their values and standards because much of their *Vibe* is emblazoned in their standards. (Some call them values and some call them standards, and some have both values and standards.)

> EVERY ORGANIZATION SHOULD HAVE CLARITY ON THEIR VALUES AND STANDARDS BECAUSE MUCH OF THEIR *VIBE* IS EMBLAZONED IN THEIR STANDARDS.

Keep your professional standards posted in every room in your building. Have your team members include them in the very first in-person interview when they're recruiting people for your firm. Tell the people being interviewed that, if you make them an offer, they'll need to know these standards are solid expectations of how we operate and they need to be sure they can live with them.

By way of example here are TJI's professional standards:

1. **Save Tony's time,** keeping him in front of and serving our clients.
2. **Kaizen,** which means constant improvement for all team members—including ongoing COEs (correction of errors), personal SWOTs, and MOLO (more of/less of) refinements.
3. Keep everything clean and **Organized**. This adds to our brand and makes us always ready.
4. Constant **List-making** ensures prioritizing, accountability, and execution of faster results (including CSFs).

5. Over-**Communicate** and calculate. This helps ensure efforts are maximized. Avoid absolutes—words like *never, always,* and *can't*—because all things are possible.

6. **Focus** efforts on new flows of business/revenue. Daily priorities include pipeline management, SOW development, and processing receivables. Remember, cash is king!

7. Do ***Favors in Advance*** **(FIA)**—sharing, giving, and helping others win.

8. **Do things now**! Operate with a mindset of quick action and speed to completion, while using *Production Before Perfection* to manage procrastination.

9. Be **Proactive** in everything (think ahead, prep ahead, do ahead, invoice ahead, deliver ahead, and exceed expectations all around—internally and externally).

10. Employ the **Team** approach—overlap, cross-support, encourage, leverage each other's expertise, and together keep all eyes on getting things done and completed, with RESULTS produced hourly, daily, and weekly.

It shows a leadership *Vibe* when an organization takes the time and has the discipline to put its standards in print and communicate them when a person is first being interviewed so they will know how the culture works. It's also important to base performance appraisals on your standards. Let your people rate themselves on how well they are operating by your standards. If you let them slide, then you let your *Vibe* slide.

IT SHOWS LEADERSHIP *VIBE* WHEN AN ORGANIZATION TAKES THE TIME AND HAS THE DISCIPLINE TO PUT ITS STANDARDS IN PRINT AND COMMUNICATE THEM WHEN A PERSON IS FIRST BEING INTERVIEWED SO THEY WILL KNOW HOW THE CULTURE WORKS.

Let me pause and give credit where credit is due. I was a partner with a consultant named Jim Million, a former pastor, for two years in 1993 and 1994. We worked together at Chrysler to help turn the company around. Jim was absolutely amazing with his passion and energy. I would watch him put his charisma to work in a room, and people would be awed. At first, I thought, *This dude is a little too far out there.* Then I came to realize that I was wrong and he was right. That's who he was, and he didn't tilt it back. I learned so much from him.

No, being "too far out there" isn't for everyone. The point of this book is to not to make you into Tony Jeary. The point is, you can take advice from people who live *Vibe*. Since then, I've intentionally brought energy and *Vibe* wherever I go, and I'm suggesting that could be a big piece of your organization's culture and your success in life.

BRING ENERGY AND *VIBE* WHEREVER YOU GO, AS THIS COULD BE A BIG PIECE OF YOUR ORGANIZATION'S CULTURE AND YOUR SUCCESS IN LIFE.

CHAPTER 7
VIPS

For the Individual: Discipline

1. Leaders with *Vibe* know where they're going, and they stay on the path to get there.
2. When you're late, it creates a negative *Vibe.*
3. Like it or not, a thin waistline contributes to your *Vibe.*
4. Keeping things clean and organized validates your *Vibe.*

For the Organization: Standards

5. Every organization should have clarity on their values and standards because much of their *Vibe* is emblazoned in their standards.
6. It shows leadership *Vibe* when an organization takes the time and has the discipline to put its standards in print and communicate them when a person is first being interviewed so they will know how the culture works.
7. Bring energy and *Vibe* wherever you go, as this could be a big piece of your organization's culture and your success in life.

CHAPTER 8 TEAM PLAYER/ *HIGH-PERFORMING TEAM* (HPT)

For the Individual: Team Player

As a leader, are you a team player? Do you set your people up to look good? Do you help them prepare ahead? Do you help them win? If you're a leader with *Vibe*, you do.

One of the benefits we offer during coaching sessions is live notetaking. The session manager takes the notes in real time, and they show up on a big screen for all to see. During a session, we may ask the session manager to pull up on the screen anywhere from three to fifteen additional documents, PowerPoint presentations, models, book covers, and anything else we've created to help me make a point. Before a session goes live, the session manager is informed what documents may be needed. That way, everything is at hand and no time is wasted searching.

LEADERS WITH *VIBE* ARE TEAM PLAYERS WHO SET THEIR PEOPLE UP TO LOOK GOOD AND HELP THEM WIN.

As a team player, how do you look out for your people? How do you show you care? Do you know what's important to your team members?

TEAM PLAYERS LOOK OUT FOR THEIR PEOPLE, SHOW THEM THEY CARE, AND KNOW WHAT'S IMPORTANT TO THEM.

One of my writers has been with me for twenty years and has probably helped me write about half of my sixty-plus titles. We often write multiple books at the same time; so when a book call is scheduled, I'm careful to consider her schedule and even negotiate more time with our coauthors when she's pressed. I believe that kind of team spirit should play out in leaders' attitudes so their people enjoy working with them.

A good leader enjoys seeing members of his or her team get recognition from others. In chapter 5 we told how the rest of our team showed their gratitude to Daniel, our general manager, for his caring attitude. Daniel deserved that recognition because he's a great example of someone who serves, and as a team player I wanted to make sure we included that in this book.

A GOOD LEADER ENJOYS SEEING MEMBERS OF HIS OR HER TEAM GET RECOGNITION FROM OTHERS.

Leaders with *Vibe* are team players—they look for ways they can support the people on their team and help them prepare ahead so they can shine and win.

For the Organization: *High-Performing Team* (HPT)

In 1995, while I was coaching the president of Ford, they commissioned me to do a special team-building project for their top executives. I wasn't a team building expert, but because they trusted me and my brand, I got the assignment. I poured a year of my life into understanding the difference between a group and a team, and I learned how to bring people together into a *High-Performing Team.* Since that time, we've positively impacted many organizations with this expertise and proved it over and over.

What is the difference between a group, a team, and a *High-Performing Team*? As we go through this, think about your own organization, whether you have six people or 6,000, and see where you fit in this model.

IN A GROUP, THE PEOPLE WORK WITH NO REALLY CLEAR COMMON GOALS OR TASKS, AND THEY EXECUTE THEIR TASKS INDEPENDENTLY. THERE'S VERY LITTLE *VIBE* IN A GROUP.

Level one in the model is the group. In a group, the people work with no clear common goals or tasks, and they execute their tasks independently. They may do fairly well in their silos and be able to make things happen, and yet they aren't fully synergized. There's very little *Vibe* in a group. Many, maybe most, organizations function at this level.

Level two is the team. It's a group of people working together interdependently toward a common goal. A team is one level above a group, yet it still is not the top level.

Where you really want to be is level three, and that's operating as a *High-Performing Team*. At this level, your people are focused on being as effective as possible. They work together to get the very best results, and they continually reevaluate to make sure they produce the best quality. Each team member has a high level of investment in the outcomes, so each individual is highly motivated.

A TEAM IS A GROUP OF PEOPLE WORKING TOGETHER INTERDEPENDENTLY TOWARD A COMMON GOAL. A TEAM IS ONE LEVEL ABOVE A GROUP, AND YET IT STILL IS NOT THE TOP LEVEL.

The energy within a *High-Performing Team* is high because its members have an eagerness to listen and collaborate in the creative process. There is a constantly ongoing, imaginative, epiphany-creating refinement within the team with the right *Vibe*. It forms a culture where everyone has a receptor mentality that says, "What am I not seeing?" A *High-Performing Team* sizzles with *Vibe*.

> In a *High-Performing Team*, people work together to get the very best results, and they continually reevaluate to make sure they produce the best quality. Each team member has a high level of investment in the outcomes, so each individual is highly motivated. A *High-Performing Team* sizzles with *Vibe*.

We teach that there are three powerful elements that make the difference in moving up through those levels: accountability, communication, and trust.

Keys to Building a High-Performing Team: ACT

1. ***A***ccountability. People do what they say they're going to do, on time or before. If you can't do something on time, you may have to renegotiate your commitment; if you don't, the synergy goes down. Accountability is what keeps synergy going.

   Measuring the results with consistent outputs is so powerful for a *High-Performing Team*. Watching and making sure you've done what you said you were going to do and putting that "X" in the box makes the team synergy go up, and accountability happens.

2. ***C***ommunication. One of the top standards in my own organization is to overcommunicate because we know the power of communication.

   Communication starts with the vision, where you're going. I once had a group in my studio, and we were talking about taking the executive team to the highest level. We recognized pretty quickly that there was a challenge from a communication standpoint.

   The owners of the organization had not defined the mission and vision for the executive management team. Because there was no real clarity about the mission and vision for the organization, they were struggling and were not able to synergize at the highest level as a team. Let me encourage you, as a leader, to ensure the vision and mission are clearly understood and cascaded all the way down in your organization.

   Also, make sure your meetings are clear, maximized, and inspiring. It is so vital for leaders to have effective meetings with defined objectives and strong agendas if they want to take their organizations to the highest level.

3. ***T***rust. People on your team will follow through if there's a high level of trust. With a culture of trust, individual expertise is valued

and respected, support is given, innovation happens, and team members are empowered. Because of the synergy that comes with trust, expectations are managed very carefully. If someone says they're going to do something, they usually do it.

> THERE ARE THREE POWERFUL ELEMENTS THAT MAKE THE DIFFERENCE IN MOVING UP THROUGH THOSE LEVELS: ACCOUNTABILITY, COMMUNICATION, AND TRUST.

If you want to bring extreme *Vibe* to your team, lead it as a *High-Performing Team*. People love to work for an organization if they know they are respected, trusted, and a part of something bigger than themselves.

CHAPTER 8
VIPs

For the Individual: Team Player

1. Leaders with *Vibe* are team players who set their people up to look good and help them win.
2. Team players look out for their people, show them they care, and know what's important to them.
3. A good leader enjoys seeing members of his or her team get recognition from others.

For the Organization: *High-Performing Team* (HPT)

4. In a group, the people work with no really clear common goals or tasks, and they execute their tasks independently. There's very little *Vibe* in a group.
5. A team is a group of people working together interdependently toward a common goal. A team is one level above a group, and yet it still is not the top level.
6. In a *High-Performing Team*, people work together to get the very best results, and they continually reevaluate to make sure they produce the best quality. Each team member has a high level of investment in the outcomes, so each individual is highly motivated. A *High-Performing Team* sizzles with *Vibe*.
7. There are three powerful elements that make the difference in moving up through those levels: accountability, communication, and trust.

CHAPTER 9
CLARITY AND FOCUS

For Both the Individual and the Organization: Clarity and Focus
Clarity, Focus, and Execution are the three elements in our foundational *Strategic Acceleration* methodology. In this chapter, let's talk about clarity and focus, as that's where the fastest and best results start for both an individual leader and an organization.

CLARITY AND FOCUS ARE WHERE THE FASTEST AND BEST RESULTS START FOR EITHER AN INDIVIDUAL LEADER OR AN ORGANIZATION.

In 2006, the president of our company interviewed our top thirty clients to find out what value they perceived they were really getting for their money. Here's what he found: "You're helping people think. Thinking is not easy. In fact, it's hard, and most people don't do it enough. You show people that the way to think better is to gain *clarity* of their visions (what they want and where they want to go), and then how they can better *focus* their efforts and the efforts of their team so they can *execute* with accountability to get the right results faster." Now, since we've had the epiphany that has led to this book, we know that *Vibe* has been the catalyst all along that has accelerated the benefits of our gift of clarity, focus, and execution to our clients.

In strategy sessions, I often ask people to rate themselves on a scale of 1 to 10 on how clear they are on where they're going with their business in the next twelve months. The answer is usually around seven. As we start showing them things they hadn't thought about regarding clarity, they often say, "Well, maybe I'm a four or a five." The same thing may happen when we ask how clear they are on their goals. They will typically show their one page of goals, and then I'll show them my 150 pages. They usually say, "Oh, I guess I'm not as clear as I could be." It's just a matter of contrast.

Clarity is about understanding your vision, outlining priorities and objectives, and tackling goals with a real sense of urgency and focus. Clarity is achieved when ideas and concepts are clearly explained and presented internally and externally, and when you know where you are in relation to where you want to go—both as an individual leader and corporately. And remember, a big part of clarity is having clearly defined values so you can make sure your values align with your goals.

CLARITY IS ABOUT UNDERSTANDING YOUR VISION, OUTLINING PRIORITIES AND OBJECTIVES, AND TACKLING GOALS WITH A REAL SENSE OF URGENCY AND FOCUS.

Without a clear vision, you're just traveling and rarely arriving. A clear vision pulls and energizes you toward getting what you want. We suggest you go as far as you can see in this fast-paced and changing world, and then you can see farther. When you get more clarity as the weeks and months go down, you can make any tweaks or changes that are needed.

Ask yourself: On a scale of 1 to 10, how clear are you and how clear is your organization?

People are attracted to leaders and organizations that have real clarity of where they're going and those who have focused their efforts on their goals. Focus is the opposite of distraction, and it is crucial for every high achiever. It takes an intentionally focused person to minimize distractions.

Focus is perhaps the ***single*** most impactful area that has the greatest opportunity for improvement for the majority of the people we fine-tune, support, and advise. Our hectic speed of life makes it easy to get sidetracked. People lose focus and often don't even realize it until they or their organizations begin to suffer. Often, the difference between someone who is successful and someone who isn't is focus. You truly do get more of what you focus on.

FOCUS IS PERHAPS THE SINGLE MOST IMPACTFUL AREA THAT HAS THE GREATEST OPPORTUNITY FOR IMPROVEMENT FOR THE MAJORITY OF PEOPLE.

One of the main subsets of focus is *High Leverage Activities* (HLAs). When people are on their game, doing the things they're really good at, and are in alignment with their job responsibilities, they're living in their *High Leverage Activities.*

So, on that same scale of 1 to 10, how focused are you as an individual and how focused is your organization? Are you tied up with constant distractions, or are you focused?

WHEN PEOPLE ARE ON THEIR GAME, IN THEIR SWEET SPOT, DOING THE THINGS THEY'RE REALLY GOOD AT AND ARE IN ALIGNMENT WITH THEIR JOB RESPONSIBILITIES, THEY'RE LIVING IN THEIR *HIGH LEVERAGE ACTIVITIES*.

Whatever level you're on with either clarity or focus, we want to help you go to another level. There are no two ways about it: Most people want to work for and with an organization that's clearly going somewhere, has its act together, and is focused on the effort it takes to get the best results with a commitment to its ownership and investors. We want you to have more of both clarity and focus so you and your organization will have more *Vibe.*

ORGANIZATIONS THAT HAVE EXTREME CLARITY AND FOCUS HAVE MORE *VIBE*.

CHAPTER 9
VIPS

For both the individual and the organization:

1. Clarity and focus are where the fastest and best results start for either an individual leader or an organization.
2. Clarity is about understanding your vision, outlining priorities and objectives, and tackling goals with a real sense of urgency and focus.
3. Focus is perhaps the ***single*** most impactful area that has the greatest opportunity for improvement for the majority of people.
4. When people are on their game, in their sweet spot, doing the things they're really good at, and are in alignment with their job responsibilities, they're living in their *High Leverage Activities.*
5. Organizations that have extreme clarity and focus have more *Vibe.*

CHAPTER 10
FLEXIBLE/BUREAUCRACY VS. STREAMLINED AND EFFICIENT

For the Individual: Flexible

Change is not a four-letter word.

In fact, being flexible and embracing change is more urgent, even essential, today than ever before. Changes and new information come at us rapidly, and a person who can shift and positively meet those changes head-on is obviously a person with *Vibe.*

> *CHANGE* IS NOT A FOUR-LETTER WORD. A PERSON WHO CAN POSITIVELY MEET CHANGES HEAD-ON IS OBVIOUSLY A PERSON WITH *VIBE.*

Sometimes change happens and we don't want to accept it. We know there's nothing we can do about it, yet we want to fight it instead of embrace it. Years ago, I got great advice from my best friend, Bill Connelly. He said, "Tony, you need to constantly be asking yourself, *Does it really matter*?" And he's right. Sometimes when we get upset about changes that are happening in our lives, we just have to stop and ask ourselves that question. When things change—for the good or for bad—the real question is, *How am I going to deal with it*? I can tell you from experience that if we make the decision to embrace the change and make the best of it, good will come from it.

> WHEN CHANGE OCCURS, DON'T FIGHT IT; RATHER, CONSTANTLY BE ASKING YOURSELF, *DOES IT REALLY MATTER?*

One of the most powerful words in the English language is *serendipity,* which is a great concept to apply when change happens. In 2013, I authored a book called *Living in the Black,* which is my autobiography of sorts. I wanted the book to have real value, so wrote it in the form of fifty-five lessons I had learned throughout my lifetime that seemed the most important. This is what I wrote about change:

> The whole idea about the powerful concept of serendipity is to *look for* the good in "happenstances" and change. Yes, I've worked hard my entire life and have lived out many significant distinctions that have brought me to the place I am today. But I can't deny that many unexpected happenstances came along that I seized opportunity from, and the results have been amazing. When the real estate and oil markets burst in the 1980s, I determined that the fallout from that—the loss of everything I had—would not destroy me. I learned from it and moved on. Then, much later in my career, happenstance eventually led me to such incredible opportunities as working with the U.S. Senate.

THE WHOLE IDEA ABOUT THE POWERFUL CONCEPT OF SERENDIPITY IS TO LOOK FOR THE GOOD IN HAPPENSTANCES AND CHANGE.

Here's how that one happened: Somehow, the Sergeant at Arms in the Senate came across the little passport booklet I published a few years ago called *Strategic Acceleration.* (It was the precursor to the full-fledged book by the same name that was published in 2009.) The Sergeant at Arms called me and asked, "Would you come and speak to our management on this concept? We really need the whole 'clarity, focus, and execution' strategy."

When I flew up to Washington, I had no idea that there are about 7,000 people who run the Senate from five different buildings (their printing department alone has about 140 people), and that there are more than 150 leaders who manage the operations

> of the Senate. I would bet most people in our country don't realize that, either.
>
> But look at what came about as a result of that engagement. What it did for me was to open my eyes to the need for clarity, focus, and execution in government, as well as in organizations everywhere. I came back so excited about that; and I told my president, Jim Norman, "Hey, I think we're on to something!" Jim's reply was, "Well, you know, I've been telling you that. That's what you do for people—you help them get really clear on what they want and help them identify the activities they need to focus on to get there." And the rest, as they say, is history. We turned that little passport into a bestselling book that would help people get better results, and now I'm spreading the word around the globe daily.

I was fascinated by the results when I started embracing the concepts of flexibility and serendipity. I can't tell you how often something in my life has changed that I thought would not end well; then I would step back and look for serendipity. I would go from being upset about the change to thinking about how it could be better. People are drawn to that kind of maximized flexibility, where they see you take a disappointment and flip it around to make it better.

There are three camps when it comes to accepting change. Most people don't like it, a few are in the middle, and the rest embrace it. Which camp are you in?

For the Organization: Bureaucracy vs. Streamlined and Efficient

When you have to say to someone, "My company is a big ship, and it's really hard to get something approved here," your organization has a negative drain of *Vibe*.

> AN ORGANIZATION THAT HAS A REPUTATION OF BEING A BUREAUCRACY WHERE IT'S HARD TO GET SOMETHING DONE HAS A NEGATIVE DRAIN OF *VIBE*. BUREAUCRACY UNDERMINES EMPOWERMENT.

When you have an organization that is streamlined in its levels of authority and is managed appropriately, lines of communication are efficient, and you can make things happen. People today love that kind of speed. Bureaucracy undermines empowerment. It slows everything down, and it causes stressed and unhappy employees.

In a *Harvard Business Review* article entitled "What We Learned About Bureaucracy from 7,000 HBR Readers," these are four of the takeaways they listed from their research:

1. Bureaucracy is a time trap.
2. Bureaucracy is the enemy of speed.
3. Bureaucracy frustrates innovation.
4. Bureaucracy feeds inertia.[2]

On the other hand, when your people have the resources, tools, motivation, and authority to do their work—and are held accountable to do so—the opposites are true. There is less time wasted, your employees can work much faster, and they are more inspired to bring fresh ideas to the table. When people are empowered to make decisions rather than having to go through several levels of bureaucracy, they feel more vested in the organization's outcomes.

When your people have the resources, tools, motivation, and authority to do their work—and are held accountable to do so—there is less time wasted, your employees can work much faster, and they are more inspired to bring fresh ideas to the table. And when people are empowered to make decisions rather than having to go through several levels of bureaucracy, they feel more vested in the organization's outcomes.

CHAPTER 10
VIPS

For the Individual: Flexibility

1. *Change* is not a four-letter word. A person who can positively meet changes head-on is obviously a person with *Vibe*.
2. When change occurs, don't fight it; rather, constantly be asking yourself, *Does it really matter*?
3. The whole idea about the powerful concept of serendipity is to *look for* the good in happenstances and change.

For the Organization: Bureaucracy vs. Streamlined and Efficient

4. An organization that has a reputation of being a bureaucracy where it's hard to get something done has a negative drain of *Vibe*.
5. When your people have the resources, tools, motivation, and authority to do their work—and are held accountable to do so—there is less time wasted, your employees can work much faster, and they are more inspired to bring fresh ideas to the table. And when people are empowered to make decisions rather than having to go through several levels of bureaucracy, they feel more vested in the organization's outcomes.

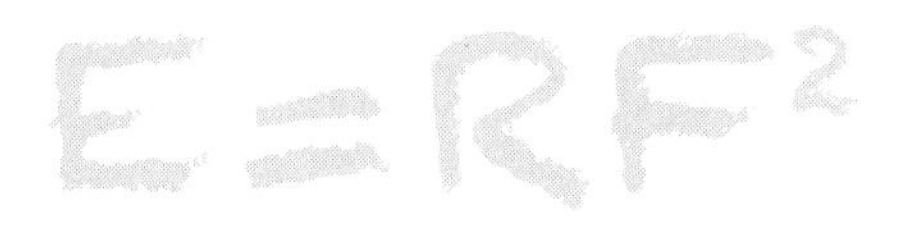

PART 3
ORGANIZATION

"Clutter is nothing more than postponed decisions."
—Barbara Hemphill, aka "The Paper Tiger Lady," Founder, Productive Environment Institute

We believe when we move into other people's spaces, we can feel their *Vibe*. Then when we do see their space, we start making judgments—often based on how organized they are in such things as:

- Their environment (home, office, and even their vehicle)
- Their dress and overall put-together appearance
- Their backpack (what they carry and how they organize their materials)

As leaders, we have an opportunity to be organized and on our game in all those areas and more in order to make the very best impact with our *Vibe*.

CHAPTER 11 EFFICIENT/BEST-PRACTICE ORIENTED

For the Individual: Efficiency

Individual efficiency creates a giant *Vibe* that others generally notice right away.

Jack Furst, my partner in our RESULTS Center building, texted me recently that he thought I was the most efficient man on the planet. That compliment meant the world to me because Jack is one of the most prominent business investors in Texas and because I put great efforts in living what we advise others to do in this area.

INDIVIDUAL EFFICIENCY CREATES A GIANT *VIBE* THAT OTHERS GENERALLY NOTICE RIGHT AWAY.

Much of what we teach is centered around efficiency. For example, we suggest that virtually anyone who can afford to hire a private driver do so today, or at least consistently use Lyft or Uber rather than driving themselves. Those who do go to another whole level in their efficiency because the extra time allows them to check emails, make phone calls, and generally stay on top of things—all while paying someone else to sit through the traffic lights. I often ask people, "If it costs $25 or $30 an hour, maybe less, to have Uber drive you, could you be making more money—and be doing what you *enjoy* doing—while you're sitting in the back seat?" If the answer is yes, then that would certainly be an example of one way they could be more efficient.

TO GO TO ANOTHER WHOLE LEVEL IN YOUR EFFICIENCY, HIRE A PRIVATE DRIVER IF YOU CAN AFFORD TO, OR AT LEAST CONSISTENTLY USE LYFT OR UBER RATHER THAN DRIVING YOURSELF.

And people take notice when you do that. When I pull up with a driver, people are often impressed that I invest in such attention to detail that I have someone in place to help me with my logistics. And we've even taken it to the extent of creating a mobile office in our RESULTS1 Van. When someone opens the door, they may see our team in there working away on their computers.

Not everyone in business needs or wants or can afford that level of efficiency. However, it certainly creates *Vibe*. In fact, we were working with a doctor just last week, and he was talking about how he had considered a Sprinter van for an office. When he saw the RESULTS1 Van, he said, "Man, that is exactly what I was envisioning!" It instantly created *Vibe* and a connection; within just a few days, he hired me to be his coach and strategist.

We've often had other people who run companies see our efficiency and be drawn to it.

The *Vibe* we put out there is very intentional because, as mentioned in my book *Advice Matters* (coauthored with Jay), you should seek advice from people (such as coaches) who have done/are doing what you want to do. Having that kind of attraction is important.

People are often curious about why I carry at least two phones, and sometimes three. Yet it sends a *Vibe* when they see efficiency in editing and working with my phones. On the other hand, there are people who see that and say just the opposite: "I wouldn't want to be *that* efficient." Or "That's not for me." And that's okay. People are in different phases of life. Not everyone wants to be that focused and *on* all the time. If you want to be a leader with impressive *Vibe*, then a high level of efficiency needs to be part of your game.

We're also intentionally efficient about keeping supplies in our vehicles. One of my key philosophies—in fact, one of my standards—is to always have several of everything (especially the smaller items) on hand so no one on the team has to run to the office supply or to the store when we run out. I keep extra supplies in my vehicles, backpack, closets, office—everywhere. That kind of efficiency sends a positive *Vibe* to people who are around me.

> Be intentionally efficient about keeping supplies (in fact, several of everything) in your vehicles, backpack, closets, office—everywhere—because that kind of efficiency sends a positive *Vibe* to people who are around you.

For the Organization: Best-Practice Oriented

One great lesson learned from coaching the executives at Walmart is that most of them have an internal concept called Correction of Errors, or COE. It simply means you're constantly looking for best practices you can put into place. If something is not working, you either create a best practice or you search for one to correct it. It's a great philosophy that can have a tremendous impact on your organization's *Vibe*.

ADOPTING CORRECTION OF ERRORS (COE) AS PART OF YOUR ORGANIZATION'S STANDARDS IS A GREAT PHILOSOPHY THAT CAN HAVE A TREMENDOUS IMPACT ON ITS *VIBE*.

When I was coaching the president of Walmart, Mike Duke, years ago, he was managing two million people, and one of his best practices was to schedule appointments on his calendar in five-minute intervals! Mike is a humble, powerful, and gifted leader. Think about his role atop a reporting structure fifteen layers deep. It was quite an interesting setup. It was very impressive that one of the largest companies in the world—and one that has the greatest logistics—was constantly looking for best practices. Yet organizations—whether they are for-profit, nonprofit, governmental, an older company, or a newer company—that strive to have best practices in place at all levels have a *Vibe* that attracts people and attracts investors. And the opposite is true as well. Organizations that don't have those best practices in place have a hard time attracting investors.

ORGANIZATIONS THAT STRIVE TO HAVE BEST PRACTICES IN PLACE AT ALL LEVELS HAVE A *VIBE* THAT ATTRACTS PEOPLE AND ATTRACTS INVESTORS.

I was commissioned years ago to go behind the scenes of the Ritz Carlton to see how they operate. I first studied their venue in Buckland, Georgia. Then a few months later I flew thirteen hours from the US to Seoul, South Korea, to complete the gig. I got out of the car, and by the time I got about a hundred feet from the hotel's front desk, people were waving to me saying, "Welcome, Mr. Jeary. We've been expecting you." I thought, *How in the world did they keep up with me, with my thirteen-hour flight, and know when I would be here*? I learned later as I was working behind the scenes that they have a best practice that allows them to do this. When guests are getting out of their vehicles, the porters look at the business-card or tag identification on their luggage, and they whisper into a small microphone that goes to the front desk, "Mr. Jeary is arriving." Having that kind of process in place, along with their many other best practices, is what gives the Ritz Carlton a *Vibe* like few others.

For many years, Ritz Carlton printed twenty-one of their best practices on a card and gave them to their new people with instructions to quickly memorize them. In recent years, they've reduced these standards down to twelve. The underlying premise of these standards is basically that ladies and gentlemen are serving ladies and gentlemen. And that's the kind of *Vibe* you hope to get when you stay in a five-star hotel like the Ritz. Model and learn from the best.

A small, yet significant, best practice we see now in many of the fine hotels is serving water with fresh fruit in it in nice glasses rather than handing out water in plastic bottles from a discount store. It's an entirely different *Vibe*. We achieve a similar *Vibe* in our organization by buying quality water and putting labels with The RESULTS Guy™ logo on the bottles. And we intentionally organize the bottles in our office refrigerator with the labels facing forward, in order like a set of soldiers; when visitors come in, they see the TJI brand instead of just seeing a generic bottle of water.

The simple truth is, if you strive to keep Ritz-Carlton-type best practices in place in your organization, you're likely at the top of your game with your *Vibe*.

THE SIMPLE TRUTH IS, IF YOU STRIVE TO KEEP RITZ-CARLTON-TYPE BEST PRACTICES IN PLACE IN YOUR ORGANIZATION, YOU'RE LIKELY AT THE TOP OF YOUR GAME WITH YOUR *VIBE*.

Chapter 11
VIPs

For the individual: Efficient

1. Individual efficiency creates a giant *Vibe* that others generally notice right away.
2. To go to another whole level in your efficiency, have a private driver if you can afford to, or at least more consistently use Lyft or Uber rather than driving yourself.
3. Be intentionally efficient about keeping supplies (in fact, several of everything) in your vehicles, backpack, closets, office—everywhere—because that kind of efficiency sends a positive *Vibe* to people who are around you.

For the organization: Best-Practice Oriented

4. Adopting Correction of Errors (COE) as part of your organization's standards is a great philosophy that can have a tremendous impact on its *Vibe.*
5. Organizations that strive to have best practices in place at all levels have a *Vibe* that attracts team members, customers, and investors.
6. The simple truth is, if you strive to keep Ritz-Carlton-type best practices in place in your organization, you're likely at the top of your game with your *Vibe.*

CHAPTER 12 ORGANIZED/ EVERYTHING IN ORDER

For the Individual: Organized

As we mentioned in the introduction to Part 3, you can often feel a person's *Vibe* just by stepping into his/her space. Then when you actually see how well-organized that person is, you're likely even more impressed. Or, that individual's *Vibe* can be greatly diminished if the opposite is true.

YOU CAN OFTEN FEEL A PERSON'S *VIBE* JUST BY STEPPING INTO HIS/HER SPACE, AND THAT INDIVIDUAL'S LEVEL OF ORGANIZATION DETERMINES WHETHER THE *VIBE* IS POSITIVE OR NEGATIVE.

Even in today's virtual world, it's important to keep things clean and organized. You need to be intentionally aware that people are still going to make a judgment—even to the extent that someone might see during a Zoom call how organized (or unorganized) your environment is. In fact, someone told me once that a news picture of a political candidate talking to a colleague on Zoom revealed his untidy desk. Those kinds of things still make an impression today. It's important to consider the visual people will see in pictures, Zoom meetings, and web photos because what they see makes a lasting impression on your *Vibe*.

IT'S IMPORTANT TO CONSIDER THE VISUAL PEOPLE WILL SEE IN PICTURES, ZOOM MEETINGS, AND WEB PHOTOS BECAUSE WHAT THEY SEE MAKES A LASTING IMPRESSION ON YOUR *VIBE*.

For the Organization: Everything in Order

When clients walk into your space and see that everything is clean and in order, it creates an immediate positive *Vibe.*

We have recently taken orderliness up to a different level in our organization, and thus increased our *Vibe.* We have created checklists for several of our processes and best practices and even had them laminated. Now, when a new person joins the team, it doesn't take him/her weeks or months to learn the process; we just hand the new person a checklist and say, "Here's how our organization works."

TAKING THE ORDERLINESS IN YOUR ORGANIZATION UP TO A DIFFERENT LEVEL ENHANCES YOUR VIBE. CONSIDER CREATING CHECKLISTS TO ENSURE ROUTINE TASKS ARE PERFORMED PROPERLY EVERY TIME.

For example, we have a checklist that ensures everything in the RESULTS1 Van will be prepped and ready when we want use it to drive to a client's business so neither Daniel nor I have to waste our time worrying about things that should have been done beforehand. When we get into the van, we want to make sure all the electronics are working, the air conditioner or the heater has brought the temperature to whatever level is comfortable, the screen is working, there is water at every chair, and there are pens available. We want to have things in order so when we walk in, we can immediately begin working, and we're not concerned that the internet doesn't work. All the technology in our system is already organized and in place so when a client steps into the van, the mobile office is ready to go. At that point, our *Vibe* increases exponentially!

Putting these processes all in order and laminating them really is extremely helpful. These lists cover all the little things we want done. We actually have a checklist for how to prepare for the day, how to prepare when a client is coming in, and how to prepare for the end of the day.

Initials	Task
	Strategic Acceleration Studio
	Ensure all the trash is out and replaced with fresh bags
	Make sure conference table is free from debris and water spots
	Make sure conference room carpet is free from debris
	All conference room chairs same height and pushed into the table
	All pens, pencils, pads, tent cards, etc. organized, restocked, and put away in conference room
	Coffee area organized, cleaned, and fully stocked
	Use stainless steel wipes to wipe down appliances if needed
	Wipe down sink and countertop
	Tidy Tony's seating area
	Restock and organize the Best Practice Closet
	Restock refrigerators with branded waters and other drinks (facing forward, lined up neatly)
	Clear flipchart and restock with markers
	Make sure leather organizers are stocked and wiped down
	Check markers to ensure they write well
	Ensure glass doors are smudge-free
	Check the bench cabinets and ensure marketing materials are stocked
	Ensure paper towel and soap dispensers are full and wiped down

Date	Task	Completed by
	Van Checklist: Before	
	Ensure van looks nice—exterior and interior wiped down	
	Ensure there are a minimum of 2 packaged VIP kits stocked	
	Ensure book cabinet is stocked with books and passports	
	Ensure we have dollar pads, RC brochures, and other marketing materials stocked	
	Ensure drink holders are filled with TJI branded water bottles	
	Ensure we have printer and printer paper	
	Ensure Wi-Fi is working	
	Turn television on	
	Ensure we have a projector and projector screen	
	Ensure remotes and cords are orderly	

Date	Task	Completed by
	Van Checklist: After	
	Restock any books that were given away	
	Restock TJI branded water bottles in each holder, facing outward	
	Restock marketing materials	
	Vacuum/dust any debris	
	Once van is backed into hangar, leave van door open	

If you make it an SOP (standard operating procedure) to automatically have things replenished, cleaned, and organized, you as the leader won't have to expend your energy ensuring that it gets done, and you can put your energy into things that are more important.

> If you make it a standard operating procedure to automatically have things in each environment replenished, cleaned, and organized, you as the leader won't have to expend your energy ensuring that it gets done, and you can put your energy into things that are more important.

CHAPTER 12
VIPs

For the individual: Organized

1. You can often feel a person's *Vibe* just by stepping into his/her space, and that person's level of organization determines whether the *Vibe* is positive or negative.
2. It's important to consider the visual people will see in pictures, Zoom meetings, and web calls because what they see makes a lasting impression on your *Vibe* as a leader.

For the organization: Everything in Order

3. Taking the orderliness in your organization up to a different level enhances your *Vibe.*
4. Consider creating checklists to ensure routine tasks are performed properly every time.
5. If you make it a standard operating procedure to automatically have things in each environment replenished, cleaned, and organized, you as the leader won't have to expend your energy ensuring that it gets done, and you can put your energy into things that are more important.

CHAPTER 13
ARSENAL/TOOL CHEST

For the Individual Leader: Arsenal
There are three basic categories of arsenals:

1. Mental
2. Hard copy
3. Electronic

Learning to use all three types of arsenals strategically will not only accelerate your ability to communicate and add value as a leader; it will also strengthen your *Vibe.*

There are three basic categories of arsenals: mental, hard copy, and electronic. Learning to use all three types of arsenals strategically will not only accelerate your ability to communicate and add value as a leader; it will also strengthen your *Vibe.*

It takes real discipline to organize things in your mind—strategically determining where they fit, what you need to use them for, and how often you will use them, as well as whether you need to remember the details or just the highlights. It's an intentional process that incorporates what I've coined *Strategic Remembering.* When you use *Strategic Remembering* to recall things you've stored in your mind—in your mental arsenal—and are able to share them, you emit a quite impressive *Vibe.*

WHEN YOU USE *STRATEGIC REMEMBERING* TO RECALL THINGS YOU'VE STORED IN YOUR MIND—IN YOUR MENTAL ARSENAL—AND ARE ABLE TO SHARE THEM, YOU EMIT A QUITE IMPRESSIVE *VIBE.*

I've written a white paper and created a very powerful video on this concept. (Google "Strategic Remembering, Tony Jeary.") In the video we share eight ways you can help ensure powerful new ideas make it into your long-term memory.

1. Choose to be exposed to only the very best materials, concepts, and ideas. Filter out clutter and things that don't matter to you. My great friend and chairman emeritus of EO (Entrepreneurs' Organization), Peter Thomas, hired me to be his coach for life a decade ago when he was seventy. Imagine this: I boarded his yacht for the first time and started digging in and helping him, and he said, "You're going to be my coach for life." He also said, "Tony, you read a lot. Bring me book recommendations that are a 10." (That means books that rate 7, 8, or 9 don't make it into his mental storage space.)
2. Repeat new learnings multiple times and in multiple ways within the first few hours of learning. This is pretty simple. When you're helping others, be creative and repeat your new learnings often. Say things like, "Let me summarize what I just said."
3. Use multimedia, with multisensory components. There are many options here. When I publish a book today, my team often creates an accompanying video of the core content to help our students really get it. We've done this with many of the books I've published in recent years.

Daniel started a new habit protocol for our assistants. Now they often pull out their phones and video record me when I'm sharing about creating a book cover, developing a PowerPoint, or building a strategy. That way they have a recording to go back and listen to, which ensures they really hear the instructions and get them into their minds. Then they can more accurately make the assignment a reality. The mind is powerful, and so are tools and processes.

4. Utilize stories. The right stories become the theater of the mind. Think, for example, of the story I just shared about my joining Peter on his yacht in No. 1 above. Stories impact.

5. Use mnemonics, acronyms, and other memory pegs. You probably know by now I've personally published dozens and dozens of books. Inside each book, I strategically create an icon, acronyms, and a variety of memory pegs so I can help my readers remember the key points. Remember the story in chapter 8 about when I was coaching the president of Ford years ago, and his company hired me to do a large team-building assignment for many of their top leaders? In fact, I remember they gave me $1 million because it was so important. Of course, at the time I was not as astute on *High-Performing Teams* as I am today, so I studied the very best authorities and research books on the subject of team building. I built the model we talked about in chapter 8 called ACT, which stands for accountability, communication, and trust. Now, decades later, it's easy to teach from the book I wrote on *High-Performing Teams* because the basic foundation for my research and everything I've written about teambuilding boils down to the acronym *ACT.*

6. When possible, relate best practices to specific, real-life application. Whether you're wanting to remember yourself or you want others to remember what you have to say, make sure it relates to the real world. Be specific. Say things like, "Here's where you could be in five years if you did . . ." Or "You could have a better outlook on life if you . . ." Or "Have you personally ever thought about . . .?" Applying best practices in real-life applications is a powerful memory tool.

7. Understand the *why*—know the benefits as well as the pain and losses from the lack of deployment. The why matters; it's the ultimate motivator.

8. We all have cameras on our phones. Take pictures of everything that matters—billboards, screens, slides, everything—and strategically store them. Make albums for everything, then review them often and keep them handy to help you learn and also to share. Sharing something often can instantly leave a positive impression—hence, give you *Vibe.*

The next type of arsenal is hard copy. In today's world, of course, we're using less hard copy and more electronic everything. However, a few people still prefer to have something tangible they can touch, such as in a magazine, because it gives credibility to the material. Also, hard copies of a document are easier to pass around in a group and/or take notes on. Of course, hard copies can always be deployed through the electronic arsenal as well.

In addition to helping you with your mental arsenal, number eight above, of course, allows you to store things in your electronic arsenal as well. Be strategic about taking pictures and storing them in an album on your phone, in Dropbox, or in some other file on your computer or on the internet. Then, what you're really doing is intentionally organizing an electronic arsenal you can use in the future. When you can pull up a picture of a poster that represents what you're talking about, instructions on how to do something, a list of ways a product can be used, or any other valuable learning, you are giving something of value. Incredible *Vibe* comes from your ability to do that. People are often very impressed when you can click a couple of keys and pull something of value up within a few seconds.

WHEN YOU TAKE PICTURES AND STORE THEM IN AN ALBUM ON YOUR PHONE, IN DROPBOX, OR IN SOME OTHER FILE ON YOUR COMPUTER OR ON THE INTERNET, YOU'RE INTENTIONALLY ORGANIZING AN ELECTRONIC ARSENAL YOU CAN USE IN THE FUTURE.

Learning to strategically use all three types of arsenals will accelerate your ability to communicate, and it will also strengthen your *Vibe*.

For the Organization: Tool Chest

One of the things that attracts people to our agency is our electronic toolbox, which includes virtually everything we've done over the past thirty-five years. In the nineties, my company was a tier-two supplier for eight major agencies (Bozell, OmniComm, Rapp Collins, Imagination from London, Carabiner, VSI, and Ross Roy), and I noticed those agencies had not really taken the time to organize their best practices and projects so they could retrieve them and reuse them. Since I was working behind the scenes in those eight agencies, I was able to take advantage of all their different kinds of systems and started assembling my own arsenal. Now, we have an arsenal that we can pull from to support accelerated results and is second to none.

Leaders who run an organization have a decision to make—how well should they build up their Dropbox, their intranet, or their learning management systems? The decision is not how big it is but how useful these tools can be. Many companies lack *Vibe* because they have so much material that it is not easy to get to. New York Life had dozens of seminars (tools) available for their agents that were not the level they wanted. They commissioned me to organize their arsenal so agents could get to the seminars more quickly and apply them to the opportunity at hand. Inaccessible knowledge has no value at all and zero *Vibe.*

LEADERS WHO RUN AN ORGANIZATION HAVE A DECISION TO MAKE—HOW WELL SHOULD THEY BUILD UP THEIR DROPBOX, THEIR INTRANET, OR THEIR LEARNING-MANAGEMENT SYSTEM SO THEIR PEOPLE CAN USE THEM?

When a company is building a website or their intranet, or any kind of internal electronic arsenal, it must be user friendly and intuitive. Steve Jobs had a phenomenal commitment to making Apple's products intuitive—so their customers didn't even have to read directions—they just worked the way their customers' minds thought they should work. When you build your arsenal, that's the way it should be sorted and organized. Ask, *What's the natural way? If you thought about it, how could you get to it and get to it quickly?* All that plays out in a person's reflection of how an organization should build its arsenal and, in the process, enhance its *Vibe.*

WHEN YOU'RE BUILDING A WEBSITE OR YOUR INTRANET, OR YOU'RE BUILDING ANY KIND OF INTERNAL ELECTRONIC ARSENAL, IT MUST BE USER-FRIENDLY AND IT NEEDS TO BE INTUITIVE.

CHAPTER 13
VIPs

For the Individual Leader: Arsenal

1. There are three basic categories of arsenals: mental, hard copy, and electronic. Learning to use all three types of arsenals strategically will not only accelerate your ability to communicate and add value as a leader; it will also strengthen your *Vibe.*
2. When you use *Strategic Remembering* to recall things you've stored in your mind—in your mental arsenal—and are able to share them, you emit a *Vibe* that is quite impressive.
3. When you take pictures and store them in an album on your phone, in Dropbox, or in some other file on your computer or on the internet, you're intentionally organizing an electronic arsenal you can use in the future.

For the Organization: Tool Chest

4. Leaders who run an organization have a decision to make—how well should they build up their Dropbox, their intranet, or their learning management system so their people can use them?
5. When you're building a website or your intranet, or you're building any kind of internal electronic arsenal, it must be user friendly and it needs to be intuitive.

CHAPTER 14
LIFE TEAM/COMPANY TEAM

For the Individual Leader: Life Team

When I wrote *RESULTS Faster!* we asked, "What are the very top lessons to help get results faster?" Lesson 20 of that book is about your *Life Team*, which is made up of the people around you, the very close circle of individuals who help you get "life" done, or who give you advice to help you make better decisions. We all have a *Life Team*, which includes our doctors, the person who takes care of our yard or cleans our house, our attorney, our CPA, our personal friends, and can even include family members. They are all a part of our lives.

YOUR *LIFE TEAM* IS MADE UP OF THE KEY PEOPLE AROUND YOU WHO HELP YOU GET "LIFE" DONE OR GIVE YOU ADVICE TO HELP YOU MAKE BETTER DECISIONS.

If you have a list of your *Life Team* organized on your phone, you can make a quick call or text to get advice and/or delegate something to get it done. And that's an impressive piece to your *Vibe* puzzle. People are impressed when you can make something happen with a click of a key on your phone. Yet, in order to do that, it takes:

1. The awareness to realize you have a *Life Team;*
2. Continually building your team with the right people, who can get things done or give you the right advice; and
3. A commitment to nourishing your *Life Team.*

If you have a list of your *Life Team* organized on your phone, you can make a quick call or text to get advice and/or delegate something to get it done. And that's an impressive piece to your *Vibe* puzzle.

When we say nourishing people, we mean sending them notes, showing them appreciation, and doing favors for them. One time, I paid for my pool maintenance man and his wife to go have dinner at the Ritz Carlson for their anniversary. I wanted to really appreciate him because he had worked for me for eight years, and any time I called him to fix my pool, he would take the call, even on weekends. That was part of his *Vibe*. And part of my *Vibe* was that if my hot tub wasn't working when someone came to my home (like my kids' friends), I could make a quick call to get it working again because of the relationship I had with that member of my *Life Team*.

I've been blessed to have had many members of my *Life Team* for decades. I've had the same attorney and the same CPA for thirty years and the same insurance guy for almost thirty years. I've also had two fantastic ladies who have helped me run my company in various capacities for almost twenty years, as well as my main writer for two decades. Having those types of longstanding relationships can be such a powerful component of your life because of the institutional knowledge they bring of how things work in your life. That's the way your *Life Team* can make you reek with value and *Vibe*.

HAVING LONG-TERM RELATIONSHIPS WITH YOUR *LIFE TEAM* MEMBERS CAN BE A POWERFUL COMPONENT OF YOUR LIFE BECAUSE OF THE INSTITUTIONAL KNOWLEDGE THEY BRING OF HOW THINGS WORK IN YOUR LIFE. THAT'S THE *WAY YOUR* LIFE TEAM CAN MAKE YOU REEK WITH VALUE AND *VIBE*.

For the Organization: Company Team (A Players)

We believe organizations attract a combination of A, B, and C Players. B Players are those who are very steady. They're not highly charged individuals; however, they are loyal, good at follow-through, and have a solid place on an organization's team. Never discount the value of the B Player. They get their jobs done and are willing to go above and beyond when called upon. B Players also save money. Turnover carries high costs; and long-term, loyal employees are worth a lot. On the other hand, C Players are those barely making it; they need to have a reality check and move up to a B Player position or find another place to work.

It's the A Players who really give an organization *Vibe*. When they walk in, they have a smile on their faces and are ready to go. They're helpful, serving, and caring. They proactively look ahead to make exceptional experiences for the client or customer—whether they're buying a service or a product or both. A Players are essential. As a matter of fact, I believe the world is drawn to people who constantly bring value, and that's what A Players do. They are always on their toes, bringing value proactively to whomever they touch.

HAVING A PLAYERS ON YOUR TEAM REALLY GIVES YOUR ORGANIZATION *VIBE*.

Whether in training or hiring or both, you want to fill your company with A Players in as many positions as possible. C Players just don't cut it. It's not that they're bad people; it may just be that they're a bad fit and/or the timing isn't right.

THE WORLD IS DRAWN TO PEOPLE WHO CONSTANTLY BRING VALUE, AND THAT'S WHAT A PLAYERS DO; THEY ARE ALWAYS ON THEIR TOES, BRINGING VALUE PROACTIVELY TO WHOMEVER THEY TOUCH.

Do you have an organized approach to bringing in the right people and integrating them into your team? Can you provide the right tools for effective onboarding of a new prospect? Do you clearly communicate your expectations and standards up front? Do you say, "If you want to join our organization, please know these are our standards; this is the way we do business." That way, you set up an A-Player mentality right up front. Most people who know they are not A Players will say, "No, I can't really give that kind of commitment."

SET UP THE A-PLAYER MENTALITY RIGHT UP FRONT BY SHOWING THE NEW EMPLOYEES YOUR COMPANY'S STANDARDS AND ASKING THEM TO COMMIT TO YOUR WAY OF DOING BUSINESS.

CHAPTER 14
VIPs

For the Individual Leader: Life Team

1. Your *Life Team* is made up of the key people around you who help you get "life" done or give you advice to help you make better decisions.
2. If you have a list of your *Life Team* organized on your phone, you can make a quick call or text to get advice and/or delegate something to get it done. And that's an impressive piece to your *Vibe* puzzle.
3. Having long-term relationships with your *Life Team* members can be a powerful component of your life because of the institutional knowledge they bring of how things work in your life. That's the way your *Life Team* can make you reek with value and *Vibe*.

For the Organization: Company Team (A Players)

4. Having A Players on your team really gives your organization *Vibe*.
5. The world is drawn to people who bring value constantly, and that's what A Players do; they are always on their toes, bringing value proactively to whomever they touch.
6. Set up the A-Player mentality right up front by showing the new employees your company's standards and asking them to commit to your way of doing business.

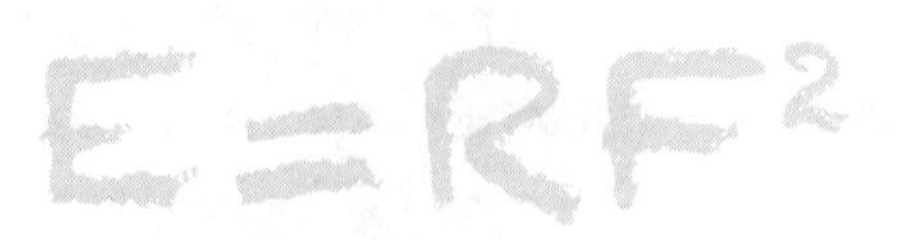

CHAPTER 15
ENERGIZED/FAST PACED

For the Individual Leader: Energized

There are several different ways you can keep your body energized. You can energize it with vitamins, caffeine, or B12 shots, or just by putting a good balance of complex carbs in your body. You need a natural flow of glucose to keep you energized and going strong. All those things play into being a person who is motivated and cheerful—a person with *Vibe* whom people want to be around and follow.

> PEOPLE WHO ARE ENERGIZED, MOTIVATED, AND CHEERFUL OFTEN HAVE A SENSE OF URGENCY, AND THEY HAVE A *VIBE* THAT PEOPLE USUALLY WANT TO BE AROUND.

Will is a new team member in our office who acts as a session manager, and we're all so impressed with the way he moves—or rather, zooms! He has boundless energy, and we can see him going into a leadership role with that one day. His sense of urgency is impressive. He gets things done quickly with a do-it-now kind of attitude. In short, he has *Vibe*!

Energized people are much more likely to be organized because that allows them to get things done more quickly. They like to operate with lists so they can maneuver through their day, make better decisions, and make things happen.

> ENERGIZED PEOPLE ARE MUCH MORE LIKELY TO BE ORGANIZED BECAUSE THAT ALLOWS THEM TO GET THINGS DONE MORE QUICKLY.

The third leg of the *Strategic Acceleration* methodology (clarity, focus, and execution) is execution. I preach every day that people who make and work from lists are the people who execute the best, and they're the ones who are energetically progressing on to the next thing. That means they're putting x's in the boxes on their lists, rather than just a slash (which indicates the task is half working and not yet finished).

PEOPLE WHO MAKE LISTS ARE THE PEOPLE WHO EXECUTE THE BEST, AND THEY'RE THE ONES WHO ARE ENERGETICALLY PROGRESSING ON TO THE NEXT THING.

On the other hand, people who are not very energetic and don't use lists sometimes get bogged down because they procrastinate or forget. They have trouble setting priorities. They're often judged as being a person who is . . . well . . . slow, or someone who is not capable of managing much work. All these things can affect a person's sales results, brand, and of course professional success, and their success translates into your success.

What kind of leader are you? Are you an energetic person with *Vibe*?

For the Organization: Fast-Paced

Being fast-paced is a cultural characteristic that comes from the top. It has to do with what you as an organizational leader demand in terms of your expectations and the way you train your people and the example you set. If you have a fast-paced, get-it-done-now kind of philosophy, then there's a *Vibe* that comes off that says, "*That's the way I am, and that's the way I excel.*" And you usually will tend to hire the kind of people who love that kind of *Vibe.*

BEING FAST-PACED IS A CULTURAL CHARACTERISTIC THAT COMES FROM THE TOP. IF YOU HAVE A FAST-PACED, GET-IT-DONE-NOW KIND OF PHILOSOPHY, THEN THERE'S A *VIBE* THAT COMES OFF THAT SAYS, *"THAT'S THE WAY I AM, AND THAT'S THE WAY I EXCEL."*

Will every person in your organization be in that fast-paced mode? It depends on the size of your organization but probably not. However, people can kick it up a notch if they know that's what is expected of them—and especially if that's what is being recognized and rewarded.

Do you recognize people who are getting things done? This morning I got up about six o'clock, and I sent my list for the day to Eloise, who is in charge of our client relations and business development. And, literally within just a few minutes of her starting her day, she had already sent back to me the portion of the list that pertained to her. So I sent back a note that said, "Thank you for your speed this morning." We've worked together for over fifteen years, and she shares my appreciation for speed; and having a shared appreciation for it is what causes a culture to have it.

A SHARED APPRECIATION FOR SPEED IS WHAT CAUSES A CULTURE TO HAVE IT.

Many people, and especially millennials, are attracted to the *Vibe* that type of culture emits. People want to take their personalities into an organization where it feels comfortable. If you want to attract people who are fast-paced, that needs to be the norm in your organization.

IF YOU WANT TO ATTRACT PEOPLE WHO ARE FAST-PACED, THAT NEEDS TO BE THE NORM IN YOUR ORGANIZATION.

CHAPTER 15
VIPs

For the Individual Leader: Energized

1. People who are energized, motivated, and cheerful often have a sense of urgency, and they have a *Vibe* that people usually want to be around.
2. Energized people are much more likely to be organized because that allows them to get things done more quickly.
3. People who make lists are the people who execute the best, and they're the ones who are energetically progressing on to the next thing.

For the Organization: Fast-Paced

4. Being fast-paced is a cultural issue that comes from the top. If you have a fast-paced, get-it-done-now kind of philosophy, then there's a *Vibe* that comes off.
5. A shared appreciation for speed is what causes a culture to have it.
6. If you want to attract people who are fast-paced, that needs to be the norm in your organization.

PART 4
COMMUNICATION

"Communication—the human connection— is the key to personal and career success."
— Paul J. Meyer

Year after year, surveys reveal that the number one item HR leaders say could be improved companywide is communication. The company that has mastered communication has a big advantage because its people feel connected, in the know, and valued. They know the company's objectives and vision, and they feel a part of something bigger than themselves. They understand that when the company wins, they win. The *Vibe* in that kind of company is almost tangible. People who work for companies that don't put the right priority on communication typically have no idea what the company's objectives are; they're often not even sure what their leaders really want or care about. *Vibe* is sadly lacking or even absent in those situations.

THE COMPANY THAT HAS MASTERED OR EVEN SEMI-MASTERED COMMUNICATION HAS A BIG ADVANTAGE BECAUSE ITS PEOPLE FEEL CONNECTED, IN THE KNOW, AND APPRECIATED. THE *VIBE* IN THAT KIND OF COMPANY IS ALMOST TANGIBLE.

High-performance companies make effective communication one of their top five standards. Yes, they run the risk that someone may read an email twice; but isn't that far better than having someone feel he or she is not in the know or letting something fall through the cracks? If something gets overlooked because of poor communication, it creates a lot of negative emotions and people get discouraged and embarrassed.

A team that is fully attuned as the ship is moving forward or new information is coming in—including a win—is able to celebrate together. If you close a deal or something else happens that's positive and it is communicated in a newsletter, a video, an all-hands-on-deck meeting, or even a simple email, it can be very powerful for both the leadership and the organization. It increases your *Vibe* exponentially.

CHAPTER 16 PRESENTATIONS/ MEETINGS

For the Individual Leader: Presentations

One giant thing that showcases your *Vibe*—or lack of it—as much as anything else is your presentations. We often use "presentation" and "communication" interactively, and together they are more than a skill set. They are a strategic asset for both an individual and an organization. How well you present matters!

We believe that "life is a series of presentations"; in fact I published a book by that title with Simon & Schuster. It became a best seller and was touted on "Shark Tank" as one of the six "must-read" business books for entrepreneurs. The message was that we're presenting all the time, both personally and professionally, and we need to know how to present well in order to win more. Whether we're a leader of our home or our organization, we're doing planned presentations, impromptu presentations, and one-on-one presentations continuously, and we're often doing group presentations, both in person and on the web. If you want your spouse to go out to dinner with you, you're going to make a presentation. It is the same if you're pitching your product.

Presentations are a big part of the communication puzzle. Some people are more gifted and can naturally bring charisma to a presentation, where others need to be a little more strategic and maximize their attention to details, such as preparation, processes, and tools. There are a number of different ways you can leverage your talents to bring *Vibe* to your presentations.

It's fairly common knowledge that many people fear public speaking more than death. As far as I know, stage fright has never killed anyone; however, it has kept people from moving forward in their careers and kept people from making valuable contributions. *Vibe* and fear are not compatible. Only by conquering your fear will you be able to bring *Vibe* into your presentations, and I'm going to give you a couple of tips on the topic to help you to do just that.

1. The most common reason people are nervous when it comes to presenting is the fact that they fear the unknown. When this fear stems from a lack of adequate preparation, it is justifiable. Therein lies the secret to conquering much of your nervousness—preparation. Preparation—taking the unknown and turning it into the known—builds confidence. Preparation pays big dividends! We talk more about preparation in chapter 18, and we show you how to prepare efficiently by using our 3-D Outline™.

2. One of the best ways to maximize your confidence and reduce nervousness is, of course, to rehearse your presentation until you could give it in your sleep. With each rehearsal, you become more comfortable and relaxed. You position yourself for *planned spontaneity*, which we talk about later in this chapter.

VIBE AND FEAR ARE NOT COMPATIBLE.

3. One of the most often overlooked pieces to the presentation puzzle is the idea of presenting *with* people versus presenting *at* people, which involves a completely different mindset. Look at it this way: When you're hosting people in your living room, you're looking them in the eye and speaking *with* them. It's no different if you're speaking to ten or a hundred or a thousand people in person or on a web call. (See my new book, *Mastering Virtual Selling)*. View your presentation as an interaction between you and your listeners—a chance for you to share ideas with each other. Maintain eye contact with as many as you can, speak to them as if you're speaking one-on-one, and engage them in the conversation from time to time. Ask questions and call on people for an answer. Give an impromptu quiz and ask for a showing of hands for each of the various choices. Show a slide (or a few) and ask for feedback. Include the "fun factor" and get them laughing. Keeping people connected and involved in your presentations brings a ton of energy and *Vibe* into the event.

ONE OF THE MOST OFTEN OVERLOOKED PIECES TO THE PRESENTATION PUZZLE IS PRESENTING *WITH* PEOPLE VERSUS PRESENTING *AT* PEOPLE.

4. Be real. Being real trumps being perfect, and it is a *Vibe* multiplier. Being real often means being vulnerable, and vulnerability actually adds to the impact.
5. Be so prepared that when someone asks a question during your presentation, you can easily and spontaneously answer because you know "above and beyond" the actual content of your presentation. That's a term we've coined called *Planned Spontaneity*, which we mentioned above. With *Planned Spontaneity*, you won't get flustered because someone caught you off guard, and you can quickly get back on track and stay on time.

Planned Spontaneity is being so prepared that when someone asks a question during your presentation, you can easily and spontaneously answer because you know "above and beyond" the actual content of your presentation.

It is amazing how far a wallflower can travel in the journey to what we've trademarked as *Presentation Mastery*™. Some people are satisfied with being good while others think great is good enough; however, if you really want your *Vibe* as a leader to soar, move to the level of mastery in your presentations. Remember, the enemy of mastery is greatness.

For the Organization: Meetings

We have found that one of the big differentiators in meetings with *Vibe* and those without it is simply knowing how to host an effective meeting. A CEO of AT&T once said that he often thought the company's core product was meetings. He then lamented that they weren't very good at them. I wonder how many CEOs would echo that sentiment. Meetings don't have to be a time killer and a means to avoid decision making. Meetings, properly organized and executed, can be an engine driving success.

In most cases, the most important indicator of a successful meeting is whether you've reached your objectives. One of the most basic things to understand about meetings is that the objectives trump the agenda. The agenda is designed to help ensure you deliver on the objectives; and when you can confirm to your participants that you did, it can create a unique, super-positive *Vibe.* Your participants feel good about being part of that meeting. (They can also celebrate that there will be no need for another meeting.) When you attend a meeting that doesn't start on time and the objectives are either not clear or are not met (or both), people can often feel a drag—just the opposite of energy.

IN MOST CASES, THE MOST IMPORTANT INDICATOR OF A SUCCESSFUL MEETING IS WHETHER YOU REACHED YOUR OBJECTIVES.

The point here is that you can have *Vibe* when people know your organization is serious about not having wasted meetings and that your meetings have standards. (If you don't yet have meeting standards, you can pull some from our book, *We've Got to Start Meeting and Emailing Like This*, or you can design them from the ground up for your own organization.)

CHAPTER 16
VIPs

For the Individual Leader: Presentations

1. One giant thing that showcases your *Vibe*—or lack of it—probably as much as anything else is your presentations.
2. *Vibe* and fear are not compatible. Only by conquering your fear of public speaking will you be able to bring *Vibe* into your presentations.
3. Keeping people connected and involved in your presentations brings a ton of energy and *Vibe* into the event.
4. If you really want your *Vibe* as a leader to soar, move to the level of mastery in your presentations.

For the Organization: Meetings

5. One of the big differentiators in meetings with *Vibe* and those without it is simply knowing how to hold an effective meeting.
6. In most cases, the most important indicator of a successful meeting is whether you reached your objectives. When you can confirm to your participants that you delivered the objectives, you can create a super-positive *Vibe*.
7. You can have *Vibe* when people know your organization is serious about not having wasted meetings and that your meetings have standards.

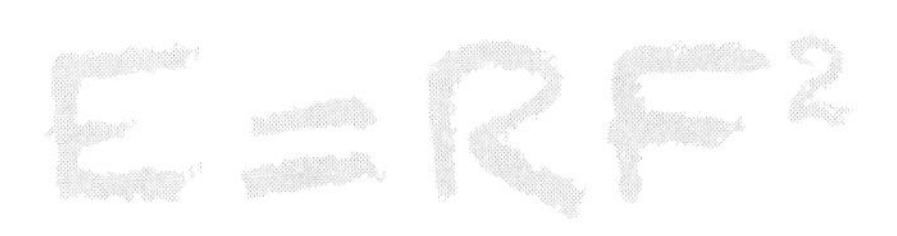

CHAPTER 17
LISTENING/SPEAKING

For the Individual Leader: Listening

Before my grandfather Smalley (whom I called Daddy Cliff) passed away, he gave me a beautiful antique telephone that he had refinished and kept in his home for many years. I have it displayed in our foyer with a plaque beside it that reminds us to "Listen well, not just talk."

LISTEN WELL; DON'T JUST TALK.

Years ago, I missed a significant opportunity because the CEO determined I didn't listen well when he interviewed me. We had been working on putting the deal together for a whole year, and I blew it when I finally had the opportunity to talk to the CEO. It was a hard lesson to learn. Obviously, our conversation was missing the *Vibe* he was looking for. I have been constantly working on improving my listening skills ever since, and I have my grandfather's phone to remind me to do that.

By being inquisitive and asking questions to help you understand better what the person you're talking to is saying—without being too interrogative—you can bring magic and an abundance of *Vibe* to a relationship. (Note: Balance being interesting with being interested.)

BRING MAGIC AND AN ABUNDANCE OF *VIBE* TO A RELATIONSHIP BY BEING INQUISITIVE AND ASKING QUESTIONS—WITHOUT BEING TOO INTERROGATIVE. (BALANCE BEING INTERESTING WITH BEING INTERESTED.)

As a leader, another great way to do that is to take notes, either on a writing pad or on your phone, when someone is talking. Whether you're on a Zoom call or meeting in person with one individual or a group, when they see you're taking notes while they're talking, they feel you're listening more.

Another big plus is to repeat back what the person said and get confirmation that you heard them correctly. For example, when Daniel and I are on a book development call with a coauthor and one of my ghostwriters, one of us will often say, "This is what I heard you say." Then we'll paraphrase what the person said and get his or her confirmation. Sometimes, though, when you paraphrase, you could miss a distinction and you need to make an adjustment. If you don't have the person confirm that you heard not only the words but also the *intent* of what he/she was saying, you might not have the *Vibe* you want in that conversation.

REPEAT BACK WHAT THE PERSON SAID AND GET CONFIRMATION THAT YOU HEARD CORRECTLY.

For the Organization: Speaking

It's critical to your brand that you bring *Vibe* to each speaking opportunity, whether you're speaking internally or externally. You may be speaking at the top of a video, on a Zoom or web call, to a large audience, on a trade show floor, or in any other environment. How well you speak and the energy, the *Vibe*, you bring could very well determine whether you achieve the outcome you're seeking. Sometimes, when you're delivering a message, you could have three different speakers—one to open the presentation, another to connect the dots, and a third to close.

HOW WELL YOU SPEAK AND THE ENERGY, THE *VIBE*, YOU BRING COULD VERY WELL DETERMINE WHETHER YOU ACHIEVE THE OUTCOME YOU'RE SEEKING.

When I was coaching the president of Walmart, Mike Duke, part of his protocol each year was speaking to all their shareholders in a stadium at their annual stockholders' meeting. Afterward he would have meetings with their analysts and institutional investors. Effectively, he was speaking on two different platforms—one to 18,000 people and the other to about 300. I was able to help him bring a great deal of *Vibe* in both instances by asking his audience members to do things like raising their hands or standing in response to his questions. In some cases we had him give members of his audience the microphone in an open forum.

Another thing Mike explored was having his team brainstorm to anticipate the questions the investors and analysts might have so they could not only have the answers prepared but also have the right person available to respond. For example, he might say, "I think I'm going to have Bob, who is our CFO, answer that question. Before I turn it to Bob, though, let me quickly mention a couple things."

That would alert Bob that Mike was about to turn it over to him and also give him a breathing space before he spoke. Mike facilitated the whole Q & A session in such a way that everyone was speaking, and no one had to talk without having a moment to think. This session was being recorded and was going all over the world, and he had a big win because he and his team were prepared and ready with the answers to their questions ahead of time. The *Vibe* that came from their team effort was masterful.

In 2004, I came out with *Life Is a Series of Presentations*. The core content of the book was eight practices to help you master presentations. There is one word that defines each of them, so I came up with the mnemonic I PRESENT.

I- **I**nvolve the audience! Engagement creates energy (*Vibe*), and facilitation is an excellent vehicle for creating engagement. Today, more than ever, people want energy. We've come to recognize that facilitation is a trump card, whether you're communicating in person or on web calls (Zoom, Skype, GoToMeeting, Team, etc.). Even electronically, you can create more energy by getting people involved, laughing, connecting, sharing, and winning, than you ever can by simply presenting your expertise. As a business leader who is knowledgeable about your industry, you can be a subject-matter expert and train, teach, and pass information along to your team; however, if you're not facilitating (versus just presenting), chances are you're not engaging them enough to really bring out the energy you may need in your organization.

Whether you're presenting virtually or in person, one example of a great way to engage your audience is to ask questions or to have people write things down. When they write things down, they get engaged. And here's another win: Their eyes go down, and you get a *Breathing Space*. In almost every speech I give, whether it's to 200 people or 20,000 people, I start with a question. So many times we talk too much, and we don't ask for involvement enough. I've learned to treasure those moments when I can simply draw a breath and reconnect.

We've discovered many other skills over the years that bring about engagement—and therefore energy—in a group. If you would like a copy of the list we've prepared, email us at info@tonyjeary.com, and we'll be happy to send it to you.

P- **P**repare your audience. Many times we invite people to a meeting or another type of presentation, and we fail to list the rich benefits they'll get when they attend. I also encourage you to touch people before you talk. If you're presenting in person, that means going out and shaking hands with the members of your audience, whether it's 10 people or 200 or 2000. If you're presenting on Zoom or another electronic space, you can visit with those who sign in early. Also, incorporate a strong *host introduction*, and then open with a solid payoff. *The first thing you say really does matter.* People start absorbing right away.

MANY TIMES IN TODAY'S WORLD, WE INVITE PEOPLE TO A MEETING OR ANOTHER TYPE OF PRESENTATION, AND WE FAIL TO LIST THE RICH BENEFITS THEY'LL GET WHEN THEY ATTEND.

R- **R**esearch and build a powerful presentation arsenal as mentioned in other parts of this book. Start with a mental arsenal of things you keep in your mind. Look around and build your arsenal with ideas you can save and use for the future. These include things you can use in an electronic arsenal—with things you have in your phone, for example—and it includes hard copy and material props, like things you can give away.

E- **E**xplain the *why*! This is so powerful, and yet people miss it all the time. Make sure to give the why by using words like *because* and *so that*. It's so important to do that in every presentation—even in your email! I might say, for example, "One of the things I encourage you to do is build an outstanding arsenal *so that* you're more content rich when you need to give a presentation."

S- **S**tate-of-mind management. If you're giving a presentation to a group of ten or more (whether virtually or in person), you will probably have all these states of mind available to you in your audience:

1. The vacationers, who are really not troublemakers; they are just vacationing.
2. The prisoners, who have their arms crossed and really don't want to be there.
3. The graduates—those people who know it all.
4. The students, who are really there to learn and absorb.

Master presenters are continually moving people to the student mentality so they want to hear what they have to say.

MASTER PRESENTERS ARE CONTINUALLY MOVING PEOPLE TO THE STUDENT MENTALITY SO THEY WANT TO HEAR WHAT THEY HAVE TO SAY.

E- **E**liminate the unknowns. Turning every unknown into the known adds confidence. I was walking through my home years ago when my oldest daughter was about ten years old and I saw her doing something that fascinated me. She had a presentation to give the next day at school, and she was preparing for it. I was blown away by what I saw, and I thought, *Man, I have to take a picture of this and use it in my work.* She was rehearsing in front of her dolls! She had heard dad talk about rehearsing and preparing, and there she was, presenting in front of her dolls.

N- k**N**ow your audience! Create a mental profile of your audience members, which could include age, background, education, and occupation. Survey your audience members ahead of your presentation through email, if possible, and talk to them one-on-one before you start your presentation (perhaps if they sign in early on Zoom or in person in your meeting space). It's important to understand your audience so you can target your objectives to meet their particular needs.

T- **T**ailor your presentation! As we've discussed in chapter 16, we developed a concept called *Planned Spontaneity*, which is being so prepared in advance that you can be flexible and ready to adjust your presentation to fit whatever issues may come up from your audience. *Planned Spontaneity* is a quality that separates the master presenters from those who are merely good.

We encourage you to study these eight concepts and use them to help you bring *Vibe* to your speaking opportunities by taking them to the highest level.

CHAPTER 17
VIPs

For the individual leader: Listening

1. Listen well; don't just talk.
2. By being inquisitive and asking questions to help you understand better what the person you're talking to is saying—without being too interrogative—you can bring magic and an abundance of *Vibe* to a relationship. (Balance being interesting with being interested.)
3. Whether you're on a Zoom call or meeting in person with one individual or a group, when they see you're taking notes while they're talking, they feel like you're listening more.
4. If you don't have the person confirm that you heard not only the words but also the *intent* of what he/she was saying, you might not have the *Vibe* you want in that conversation.

For the Organization: Speaking

5. How well you speak and the energy, the *Vibe,* you bring could very well determine the success of the outcome you're looking for.
6. Study the eight I PRESENT concepts and use them to help you bring *Vibe* to your speaking opportunities by taking them to the highest level:

I – **I**nvolve the audience

P – **P**repare your audience

R – **R**esearch and build a powerful presentation arsenal

E – **E**xplain the why

S – **S**tate-of-mind management

E – **E**liminate the unknowns

N – k**N**ow your audience

T – **T**ailor your presentation

CHAPTER 18
TIMELY, PREPARED/ AHEAD OF NEWS AND DIRECTION

For the Individual Leader: Timely, Prepared

Time is precious, and most people don't frame their time as well as they should. For example, if you're communicating on the phone, say, "I think we can accomplish our objectives for the call in eight minutes." Your phone tells you how long you've invested on each call, so look at your phone to see if you've invested the number of minutes allotted. In order for you to be better able to set a time limit for your calls, you must really know your objectives. Jot them down, or engage in a little self-talk to ensure you have them in your mind before you make the call.

KNOW YOUR OBJECTIVES AHEAD OF EACH CALL YOU MAKE SO YOU CAN STAY ON TRACK WITH YOUR TIME AND PROVIDE ENERGY TO YOUR CALL.

Leaders who manage the time factor of their communications, both in reference to how long they take and the timing of when they deliver them, exude *Vibe* to their listeners. Depending on the type of your organization, sometimes having a Monday morning communication can set up the whole week. Or, you may think a daily huddle with your team each morning is the most effective use of your (and your team's) time. Determine the timing and type of communication that's best for your organization, and be sure to determine your objectives ahead of time.

DETERMINE THE TIME AND TYPE OF COMMUNICATION THAT'S BEST FOR YOUR ORGANIZATION, AND BE SURE TO DETERMINE YOUR OBJECTIVES AHEAD OF TIME.

Years ago we developed a program and software tool that is beneficial to taking control of both the issues of time and preparedness. With our 3-D Outline™, you can break down a more formal type of communication into the minutes you want to assign to each of the items (the "what") on the agenda for your presentation. You are also prompted to assign a "why" to each item, which is the objective that item supports. This helps ensure that each topic aligns with the objectives you've set for your presentation. The outline also allows you to define "how" you will present each item (use a verbal presentation, a PowerPoint, a quiz, a prop, etc.). The elements of "what, why, and how" are the three dimensions that support the name—the 3-D Outline™. It's a powerful tool that both shortens the planning process and ensures every minute is maximized.

We've included our 3-D Outline™ template below:

THE 3-D OUTLINE™

<table>
<tr><td colspan="4">Presentation Title</td><td colspan="2">Delivery Date</td></tr>
<tr><td colspan="4">Audience</td><td colspan="2">Start Time</td></tr>
<tr><td colspan="4">Objectives</td><td colspan="2">End Time</td></tr>
<tr><td colspan="6">Final Preparation Checklist</td></tr>
<tr><td>#</td><td>Time</td><td>What</td><td>Why</td><td>How</td><td>Who</td></tr>
<tr><td>1.</td><td></td><td></td><td></td><td></td><td></td></tr>
<tr><td>2.</td><td></td><td></td><td></td><td></td><td></td></tr>
<tr><td>3.</td><td></td><td></td><td></td><td></td><td></td></tr>
<tr><td>4.</td><td></td><td></td><td></td><td></td><td></td></tr>
<tr><td>5.</td><td></td><td></td><td></td><td></td><td></td></tr>
<tr><td colspan="6">Total Time</td></tr>
</table>

Before all your meetings, think about what you're going to say, when you're going to say it, and how much passion and energy you're going to say it with.

For the Organization: Ahead of News and Direction

As the leader of your organization, you want to make sure you're communicating to your people ahead of any news or new direction that affects any aspect of your company. After all, their lives are going to be affected. Share your vision, share your ideas, and even share the possibilities to keep the energy high. When your people hear through the grapevine something of importance that affects their work, it can sometimes create a negative *Vibe*. Communicating the news and any new direction the company is going in a timely manner gives you and your organization a powerful space for positive *Vibe* because your people feel they are a part of the team and are always in the know.

MAKE SURE YOU'RE COMMUNICATING TO YOUR PEOPLE AHEAD OF ANY NEWS OR NEW DIRECTION THAT AFFECTS ANY ASPECT OF YOUR COMPANY.

Timely communication can also apply in other ways. For example, when you're working with your sales force, letting them know the status of a new product, a new offering, or the opening of a new country at just the right time can be very important. Letting them know bad news is also important. Remember, bad news doesn't improve with age. Be up front. Let them hear it from you first, along with your plans for managing the situation. This shows you trust them and assures them that they are all valued team members.

KEEPING YOUR VENDORS INFORMED ALLOWS THEM TO PROVIDE SERVICES THAT ALIGN WITH YOUR COMPANY'S PRIORITIES, STANDARDS, AND DIRECTION.

This applies to your vendors as well. When we were working with American Airlines after Doug Parker took over as their president, he would bring in all the company's advisors and consultants and share with us things that were important to him at that time as the president. Then when we coached his people, everything we said would be in alignment with his priorities, standards, and direction. He kept us ahead of the game instead of letting us hear those things that were important to him later.

CHAPTER 18 VIPs

For the Individual Leader: Timely, Prepared

1. Jotting down your objectives before you make each call helps you stay on track with your time and can help add momentum, hence energy (*Vibe*) to your call.
2. Leaders who manage the timeliness of all their communications, both in reference to how long they take and the timing of when they deliver them, exude *Vibe* to their listeners.
3. Determine the time and type of communication that's best for your organization and be sure to determine your objectives ahead of time.
4. The 3-D Outline™ is a powerful tool that both shortens the planning process and ensures every minute spent in a meeting is maximized. It can also help build momentum more clearly for your message.

For the Organization: Ahead of News and Direction

5. Communicating in a timely manner the news and any new direction the company is going gives you and your organization a powerful space for positive *Vibe* because your people feel they are a part of the team and are always in the know.
6. Keeping your vendors informed allows them to provide services that align with your company's priorities, standards, and direction. Sharing with them things that are important to you as the leader enables them to provide their services in alignment with your priorities, standards, and direction.

CHAPTER 19
ALWAYS IMPROVING/ SHARPENING THE COMMUNICATION SAW

For the Individual Leader: Always Improving

One way to constantly improve your communication is to constantly seek feedback from your team as to what you could have done better. Then turn it around and see what your team members think they could have done better. Did it do the right amount of research? Was preparation thorough? What about delivery?

In chapter 11 we mentioned Walmart's best practice of correction of errors (COEs). It's more than just a best practice though; *Kaizen* is also one of the standards for our company. *Kaizen* is a Japanese word—actually, it's a Japanese business *philosophy* of continuous improvement. We have adopted that philosophy and applied that standard of constant improvement for all team members. Kaizen includes many things, of course, like ongoing COEs, personal SWOTs, and MOLO (more of/less of) refinements. And we constantly focus on improving communication—both personally and professionally—with each other, with our clients, with our families, and even with our vendors. We've taught these best practices of self-improvement, including in the area of communication, to our clients over the years as well.

> *KAIZEN*—A JAPANESE PHILOSOPHY OF CONTINUOUS IMPROVEMENT—SHOULD BE ONE OF YOUR STANDARDS, ESPECIALLY IN THE AREA OF COMMUNICATION, IF YOU WANT TO IMPROVE YOUR *VIBE*.

We believe when people see that you, as a leader, are open to improve as a communicator, you gain *Vibe* points. They're often impressed that you've built yourself up over time to become a leader, and yet you're still always improving—you're constantly reading, studying, watching videos, benchmarking others, learning from your own mistakes, and perhaps even being coached in the area of communication. It's impressive when you never stop learning and becoming better.

For the Organization: Sharpening the Communication Saw

Our job at Tony Jeary International is to sharpen saws—and communication is one saw we sharpen often. For many top executives, sharpening their own communication saw and those of the people on their team is a blind spot. They don't see that communication is an asset rather than just a skill, and they miss the fact that great communication can bring so much *Vibe* to their organization. They often fall short of the results they want because they're not sharpening the saw. Many don't even teach their people the most simple, basic communication skills like meeting and email effectiveness.

FOR MANY TOP EXECUTIVES, SHARPENING THEIR OWN COMMUNICATION SAW AND THOSE OF THE PEOPLE ON THEIR TEAM IS A BLIND SPOT.

If you have standards that reinforce your commitment to communication mastery in your organization, and you teach people from the day they come aboard how your communication priorities and standards should be practiced, we believe you'll see a dramatic increase in your organization's *Vibe.* Weak meetings = weak *Vibe.*

Take on the mantle of constantly sharpening your own and your team's communication saws. That could include such things as consistently doing debriefs after major events as well as sending out surveys to the participants and making adjustments according to their input. It should also include bringing in subject-matter experts to teach communication skills. Whatever it takes, the impact on your *Vibe* will be worth it!

> Sharpening the communication saw in your organization could include things like debriefing after major events, making adjustments according to input from participant surveys, and bringing in subject-matter experts to teach communication skills.

CHAPTER 19
VIPs

For the Individual Leader: Always Improving

1. *Kaizen*—a Japanese philosophy of continuous improvement—should be one of your standards, especially in the area of communication, if you want to improve your *Vibe*.
2. When people see that you, as a leader, are open to improve your communication skills, you gain *Vibe* points.

For the Organization: Sharpening the Communication Saw

3. Many top executives don't see that communication is an asset rather than just a skill, and they miss the fact that great communication can bring so much *Vibe* to their organization. They're often falling short of the results they want because they're not sharpening the saw.
4. If you have standards that reinforce your commitment to communication mastery in your organization, and you teach people from onboarding forward how your communication priorities and standards should be lived out, you will see a huge increase in your organization's *Vibe*.

CHAPTER 20
EMAILING AND TEXTING/ EMAILING AND STYLE

For the Individual Leader: Emailing and Texting

Setting standards around emailing and texting can sound trivial. Yet, when they are poorly managed, their potential for creating problems is immense. Emailing and texting are two excellent tools for communicating quickly, and we believe what really gives *Vibe* to your emailing and texting is your speed. What people appreciate is your speed in getting back to them. For example, if my main writer is not available when I call, she texts me right away to let me know when she can talk. We feed off that kind of connection because we appreciate each other's time.

PEOPLE MAY LET YOU SLIDE A LITTLE ON YOUR SPELLING ON EMAILING AND TEXTING; WHAT THEY REALLY ENJOY, THOUGH, IS YOUR SPEED IN GETTING RIGHT BACK TO THEM.

We believe it is important to your *Vibe* as a leader that you respond quickly—not just to calls, but to emails and texts as well. Getting right back with people after they send you a message speaks volumes about the importance you put on your relationship with them and your appreciation of their time. We understand it's not always feasible to check your email every few minutes and respond; however, getting back with people at least within a few hours, or especially before the end of the day, shows your diligence and dependability and increases your *Vibe*. People appreciate speed. When you don't respond in a timely manner, it often creates a negative *Vibe*.

NOT RESPONDING IN A TIMELY MANNER TO TEXTS AND EMAILS CREATES A NEGATIVE *VIBE*.

Here are a couple of tips that will not only help you create emails faster; they will also help the recipient read them faster (a great way to create instant *Vibe*!).

1. Keep your messages short, sweet, and to the point. People today are really not into reading an email that looks like a letter. Rather than writing in long paragraphs, use bullets and one-liners. Your recipients will love this, because they can see in clear, succinct bullets the information you're giving them or what you're asking them to do.
2. Take advantage of the subject line; if your message is really short, it can serve as your subject! One caveat here: Make sure it's not so short and abbreviated that your recipient has no idea what you are talking about.

For the Organization: Emailing and Style (Training for Email Efficiency)

Email can be a significant time, money, and productivity drain for you and your organization if you don't learn how to make it work for you rather than against you. You need to set email standards for your organization, and they should be part of your training as well as your onboarding so your people will know what to expect. Setting and maintaining email standards is a piece of the communication puzzle that gives you an extra edge and increases your organization's *Vibe.*

EMAIL CAN BE A SIGNIFICANT TIME, MONEY, AND PRODUCTIVITY DRAIN FOR YOU AND YOUR ORGANIZATION IF YOU DON'T LEARN HOW TO MAKE IT WORK FOR YOU RATHER THAN AGAINST YOU.

We have an entire training on email, based on our book *We've Got to Start Meeting & Emailing Like This!* The book lists ten email standards for dealing with both inbound and outbound email.

1. Keep your inbox clean, current, and organized.
2. Answer emails promptly, within one business day (sooner, if possible).
3. Know your desired outcomes before you start writing and ensure your email contributes to achieving your objectives.
4. Include the appropriate people; carefully consider CCs and BCCs.
5. Clearly state the topic and desired action in the subject line and use the "urgent" indicator sparingly.
6. Be brief, clear, and direct, and use a courteous, positive, business-like tone.
7. Stop and think, remembering that what you write is permanent and may become public.
8. Optimize the layout for easy reading.
9. Use a signature block with full contact information on both messages and replies.
10. Use a personal email account for non-work-related messages.

You may want to use these standards or create your own; however, once your leadership team agrees on the basic guidelines, the standards must be communicated organization-wide. They should be posted on the company intranet and constantly reinforced through ongoing training and new-employee orientation. Remember that simply setting and communicating standards is not enough. To make an impact and create *Vibe*, the standards must be lived every day. When senior leadership not only supports but also *models* the standards, it sends a clear and compelling message to the rest of the organization to get onboard.

WHEN SENIOR LEADERSHIP NOT ONLY SUPPORTS BUT ALSO *MODELS* THE STANDARDS, IT SENDS A CLEAR AND COMPELLING MESSAGE TO THE REST OF THE ORGANIZATION TO GET ONBOARD.

CHAPTER 20
VIPs

For the Individual Leader: Emailing and Texting

1. What really gives *Vibe* to your emailing and texting is your speed; people really enjoy your getting right back with them.
2. Keep your messages short, sweet, and to the point.
3. Take advantage of the subject line; if your message is really short, it can serve as your subject!

For the Organization: Emailing and Style

4. Setting and maintaining email standards is a piece of the communication puzzle that gives you an extra edge and increases your organization's *Vibe*.
5. Once your leadership team agrees on your basic guidelines, the standards must be communicated organization-wide. They should be posted on the company intranet and constantly reinforced through ongoing training and new-employee orientation.
6. Simply setting and communicating standards is not enough. To make an impact and create *Vibe*, the standards must be lived out every day.

PART 5
STYLE

Style isn't just about what you wear; it's about how you live.
—Lilly Pulitzer, Fashion Designer

Style is an interesting word to describe. People can often look at your style and be thinking about your speed. How fast are you? How big is your sense of urgency?

Others may look at your style and consider how organized you are—how you are put together and coordinated.

Other people could look at your demeanor. Are you caring? Do you smile often? Do you show up for a meeting on time and with a good attitude?

And on the organization side, people may be wondering if you run an all-hands-on-deck kind of company where everyone pitches in to help. Is your organization welcoming when someone comes in? Do people like coming into your space, whether they work there or are just visiting? Does the atmosphere foster fun—where people can joke around and express their quick wit?

In a way, you could say that style is sometimes synonymous with *Vibe*. When someone asks, "How is this person's *Vibe*?" they could just as easily ask, "How is their style?" The two words have enough of an interchangeable distinction that they could very well be synonyms, or at least cousins.

CHAPTER 21
BUTTONED UP AND PREPARED/ EVERYTHING IN ITS PLACE

For the Individual Leader: Buttoned Up and Prepared
People who are buttoned up and prepared are typically ready. When someone (or something) unexpectedly comes into their lives, they're ready to deal with it. Some might say I'm extreme. I am. I like creating wins for people, so I often go all out. Let me share a few personal examples to perhaps push your thinking.

PEOPLE WHO ARE BUTTONED UP AND PREPARED ARE TYPICALLY READY TO DEAL WITH ANYONE (OR ANYTHING) THAT COMES INTO THEIR LIFE UNEXPECTEDLY.

Here's an example: Byson, one of our clients, came to the RESULTS Center last weekend. He had been wanting to get on my calendar, and with my busy schedule, I hadn't been able to give him the time he was requesting. Since he enjoys exercising, I suggested he come over and work out with me on Saturday. He surprised me when he showed up with his three-year-old son, Colton. When they walked in, I bent down and asked his son, "What's your name?" He wouldn't respond, so I said, "Surely you have a name. Why don't we call you 'little man'?"

His dad laughed. I took the young boy into my office and showed him a Quincy ball I had ordered for my yoga session the next day. Bison told me his son's name was Colton, so I took a magic marker and wrote "Colton" on the rubber ball. Then I handed it to him and said, "Here, this is yours."

Colton's dad Bison was impressed with that very small gesture. He sent me this text later: "Hey, bud, thank you for being so amazingly kind to my son. It speaks volumes to who you are as a human." I sent a text back saying, "God has blessed me, and my gift is encouragement— for all ages, all the time. Thanks for the note." And his reply was: "Well, you have been an amazing encourager and mentor for me and a very good friend. Thank you."

I created multiple wins by giving away a $20 yoga ball. It was easy for me to buy another one, and yet this little kid was able to walk away with something that likely caused him to say, "Wow, Dad, that was really fun!" And it probably expanded the *Vibe* I had with my client.

I wasn't necessarily prepared to give my yoga ball to Colton before he came in that morning. What I was prepared to do, though, was to find a way to make the best of any unexpected situation, and I made a little guy (and his dad) happy in the process.

I WASN'T NECESSARILY PREPARED TO GIVE MY YOGA BALL TO COLTON BEFORE HE CAME IN THAT MORNING. WHAT I WAS PREPARED TO DO, THOUGH, WAS TO FIND A WAY TO MAKE THE BEST OF ANY UNEXPECTED SITUATION, AND I MADE A LITTLE GUY (AND HIS DAD) HAPPY IN THE PROCESS.

Part of your DNA should be to always be prepared. I keep a silver box in my RESULTS hangar filled with gifts just for kids. About two months before, a group of five kids about Colton's age had come to the RESULTS Center. When these kids made an impromptu visit on a Saturday morning, I brought out the silver box and gave them each a box of collector coins from around the world; the kids loved them.

Here's another example. I recently completed my second hangar. My first is the RESULTS Hangar at the back of the RESULTS Center that houses the

RESULTS1 Sprinter Van. My second hangar is the Lakeside Hangar that's on the bottom floor of our condo at Lakeside DFW. (Google "Tony Jeary Hangar" and watch the short video). The hangar is an 1,800-square-foot, six-lane garage that will actually hold an F35 if you set it in it just right. As I was completing the hangar, I had several colleagues, mentors, and friends do a walkthrough with me to see if anything was missing, *Vibe*-wise. I'm constantly asking for insight or blind spots so that I can improve. Do you? One of my mentors suggested my bar area was too picture perfect and needed to be more welcoming and user-friendly. He was right, so I bought an ice maker and arranged it with glasses on a black rubber bar pad and put drink pourer stems in the bottles instead of caps or corks to make it . . . well . . . more friendly. As it turned out, that's the style I wanted rather than a bar setup that was so in line that it was not inviting. Then I decided to display my fifty-plus year-old Hot Wheels collection from my childhood, and I bought dozens of newer, less expensive versions to go with it. The Hot Wheels filled up one entire side of a wall; so now when kids come over, I can not only show them my collection, I can easily pull some of the newer ones off the shelf and share a gift. It's amazing how strategic preparation can be part of your style.

Prepare ahead. Be welcoming and giving.

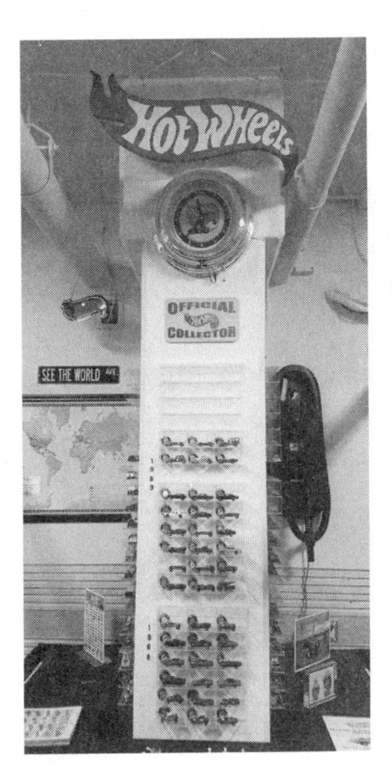

A leader who is prepared at all times exudes a *Vibe* that says, "This is a person who plans ahead and can be trusted more to deal wisely and compassionately with the unexpected."

For the Organization: Everything in its Place

There's an incredible *Vibe* that comes with having a place for everything and everything in its place. We've mentioned earlier that keeping everything clean and organized is one of our company standards; and as a result, when people walk in to the RESULTS Center, they experience that clean and organized *Vibe.*

THERE'S AN INCREDIBLE *VIBE* THAT COMES WITH HAVING A PLACE FOR EVERYTHING AND EVERYTHING IN ITS PLACE.

My grandfather owned a gas station; and besides teaching me to give service, he taught me that when people came to our station, they should see that we had all the equipment next to the pumps organized, in good shape, and in place. We had the tires rolled out. We had the wiper blades all organized. We had the windows clean, and everything was in place. We were ready for customers, for any situation. It was a lesson I learned well and kept with me for the rest of my life.

Then when I was sixteen, I started selling shoes. I had two different managers, and both of them also reinforced the importance of having everything in place. They taught me how to keep all the shoes in order and how to display them in a very organized way in the windows. Keeping everything in place was part of that company's *Vibe*, just as it was my grandfather's— and just as it is mine. Should it be yours as well?

KEEPING EVERYTHING IN PLACE SHOULD BE PART OF YOUR ORGANIZATION'S *VIBE.*

If you're not naturally inclined with the habit or the discipline to keep things organized, we have good news for you. It's the same advice we give our clients when we're teaching them new habits—you can staff for it or solve it with processes or technology. Here's what we mean: You can hire people to do it or you can create processes (like a checklist or steps to follow—see chapter 12) that make it easier to delegate tasks to someone who has more of a strength in that area. Or you can even contract it out. You can also accommodate your weakness in this area with technology. As technology continues to advance, companies are attempting to solve problems by creating apps and software, and they get paid for making things quicker, easier, and more effective. That's why they build them, so you want to make sure you look for ways you can use technology to your fullest advantage. As an example, EverNote is an app that helps you organize your notes; there are also password apps for organizing your codes, as well as tons of other ways technology can add to your preparation.

Vibe is not something you bring out of the closet when someone shows up with no advance warning. When your organization has everything in order, you don't have to worry about people coming in unexpectedly. Your *Vibe* is pretty much in place 24/7 and ready for anyone and anything.

CHAPTER 21
VIPs

For the Individual Leader: Buttoned Up and Prepared

1. People who are buttoned up and prepared are typically ready to deal with anyone (or anything) that comes into their life unexpectedly.
2. A leader who is prepared at all times exudes a *Vibe* that says, "This is person who plans ahead and can be more trusted to deal wisely and compassionately with the unexpected."

For the Organization: Everything in Its Place

3. There's an incredible *Vibe* that comes with having a place for everything and everything in its place.
4. If you're not naturally inclined with the habit or the discipline to keep things organized, you can often staff for it or solve it with processes or technology.
5. *Vibe* is not something you bring out of the closet when someone shows up with no advance warning. When your organization has everything in order, you don't have to worry about people coming in unexpectedly. Your *Vibe* is pretty much in place 24/7 and ready for anyone and anything.

CHAPTER 22
CALM/PEACEFUL

For the Individual Leader: Calm

This is one I've had to work on over the years. Who would you rather work with or for: someone who stays calm in stressful situations, thinks things through clearly, and steers the ship with determination or someone who becomes obviously rattled and irritated and kicks the furniture? People prefer calm.

This is one area of *Vibe* everyone should work on. One of the things I have admired in certain leaders over the years is their ability to stay calm. Things change and issues pop up—people don't follow through, don't show up for meetings, don't meet deadlines, come in late, or have family emergencies. When you have people working for you, you have to contend with their challenges. Being able to calmly deal with those issues by having an amicable discussion is a powerful attribute in a leader's *Vibe*. Those who do are far more likely to inspire trust and loyalty among their people. Their people know where they stand with them, and they appreciate their leader's ability to lead the company forward no matter the circumstances. When you have a calmness that allows you to perform well under pressure, you're able to think more clearly and choose your actions more carefully.

> BEING ABLE TO CALMLY DEAL WITH THE ISSUES THEY FACE BY HAVING AN AMICABLE DISCUSSION IS THE ATTRIBUTE OF A LEADER. THOSE WHO STAY CALM ARE FAR MORE LIKELY TO INSPIRE TRUST AND LOYALTY AMONG THEIR PEOPLE.

Another challenge is a side effect of our current technology, and staying calm is key. If you are in a meeting and your client is continually distracted by their Apple watch, how do you respond? You do not want to act offended, yet your focus needs to stay on the subject matter you are presenting. You need to be able to proceed in a steady manner and be prepared to backtrack, should you lose your client's attention at any point. You should practice your presentation with the assumption that the client will interrupt you at any minute. If you seem upset or angered by your clients' disengagement, you may push them away and lose the business. Keeping a calm demeanor is critical.

How well do you manage your emotions?

How well do you manage your emotions?

Whether you have a naturally calmer *Vibe* than others or you're a leader who is compulsive, anxious, or prone to anger, this is a trait you must learn to work on every day (as I do). As a leader who is charged with the many responsibilities of running a company, you may be tempted to think the world revolves around you. Know this: it doesn't. With that understanding, you'll become less demanding and better able to calmly empathize with your people and guide them toward your company's goals.

> As a leader who is charged with the many responsibilities of running a company, you may be tempted to think the world revolves around you. Know this: it doesn't.

You may remember what my best friend of thirty-five years, Bill Connelly, told me that has gone a long way toward helping me stay calm under pressure. He said, "When things are not going like you want them to, ask yourself, *Does it really matter*?" There have been many times over the years that asking myself that question has had a powerful, calming effect on me. You should try it.

Another calming technique to adopt is simple and natural: breathe. In present times, practicing tranquility has become a personal trend today, though it can also be carried over into the business arena. The power of meditation should not be overlooked. Training yourself to achieve a mentally clear and emotionally calm state is of great value toward attaining success and creating *Vibe.* If you find yourself upset over a specific task, or are unable to move forward in your thinking, take a step back. Walk around the room to clear your head, or take in a handful of breaths, holding each one for seven seconds before exhaling. Earlier we mentioned the client who was distracted by the Apple watch and dealing with distractions; however, this watch, along with other similar products on the market, can be a great tool for helping you remain calm. It can be used to remind you when to breathe and when to walk around, and it will keep track of your personal fitness goals. If you are consistently forgetful of doing these activities, you may want to invest in one of these products that will ultimately prompt you to reclaim your attention and awareness.

For the Organization: Peaceful

When you enter an organization, whether in person or virtually, your sensory acuity (the ability to use your five senses to make accurate observations) kicks in, and you're often able to discern the atmosphere, the *Vibe*, of that organization. If the *Vibe* is peaceful and stress-free, it's probably because things are organized and in order and progress is being made. You can likely feel the team synergy, which comes from people being prepared and willing to work together and help each other to support the company's vision.

> If the atmosphere of an organization is peaceful and stress-free, it's probably because things are organized and in order. You can likely even feel the team synergy, which comes from people being prepared and willing to work together and help each other to support the company's vision.

The peacefulness of an organization projects a great *Vibe*. In companies where there is dysfunction, stress, and chaos, where people are racing about in a panic to get things done, there is a negative *Vibe*.

THE PEACEFULNESS OF AN ORGANIZATION PROJECTS A GREAT *VIBE*.

When you walk from the parking lot into the front door of one of our clients we mentioned earlier, a company called Vari (formerly VariDesk),

you immediately feel peaceful. It's obvious that they have carefully thought through how to create that atmosphere. They actually engaged an acoustical engineer to come in and help them; and as a result, one of the things they did was invest in white noise machines to control the amount of background noise in the building. They had the noise machines installed in the ceiling, and it creates a very soothing, peaceful effect. Their *Vibe* is amazing.

A Harper & Hill article entitled, "The Workplace Future: Creating a Peaceful Work Environment" says:

> Human beings are a lot more sensitive to their environment than they may seem. The effect of the environment has changed how people behave, from social epidemics in society to personal lifestyle habits. Even corporations have taken advantage of the influence that the physical environment has for a successful change in the management process.
>
> The workplace environment affects how employees feel about their job and can influence their work habits. The physical environment is one factor that can affect employee productivity; it also plays a role in the work climate, depending on how the staff members interact and how they are treated. A healthy workplace environment improves productivity and reduces costs related to absenteeism, turnover, worker's compensation, and medical claims.[3]

The article went on to say that there are four aspects to look into when creating a healthy workplace:

1. workplace culture,
2. physical environment and occupational health and safety,
3. health and lifestyle practice, and
4. a supportive workplace environment.[4]

Most of these distinctions are probably even more applicable today in light of the increased stress our society is facing. For the health and wellbeing of your people, make it a point to create a peaceful atmosphere and *Vibe*, whether you're operating virtually or in an office environment.

CHAPTER 22
VIPs

For the Individual Leader: Calm

1. Being able to calmly deal with the issues they face by having an amicable discussion is a very powerful attribute in a leader's *Vibe*. Those who do are far more likely to inspire trust and loyalty among their people.
2. When you have a calmness that allows you to perform well under pressure, you're able to think more clearly and choose your actions more carefully.
3. Whether you have a naturally calmer *Vibe* than others or you're a leader who is compulsive, anxious, or prone to anger, this is a trait you must learn to work on every day.

For the Organization: Peaceful

4. When you enter an organization, whether in person or virtually by Zoom, your sensory acuity (the ability to use your five senses to make accurate observations) kicks in and you're often able to discern the atmosphere of that organization.
5. If the atmosphere is peaceful and stress-free, it's probably because things are organized and in order. You can likely even feel the team synergy, which comes from people being prepared and willing to work together and help each other to support the vision.
6. For the health and wellbeing of your people, make it a point to create a peaceful atmosphere and *Vibe*, whether you're operating virtually or in an office environment.

CHAPTER 23 PRESENCE/FIRST IMPRESSION

For the Individual Leader: Presence

What specifically do you want people to remember about you? And we're not just talking about your brand or your personality. It has more to do with your presence. We call it your *strategic presence*, and it has a unique impact on how people will follow your lead. Make it strong. Your *strategic presence* invokes a certain image that causes people to see you as a particular kind of person. Your trademark expression, style, or persona makes you memorable—or not.

WHAT SPECIFICALLY DO YOU WANT PEOPLE TO REMEMBER ABOUT YOU AS A LEADER?

Have you ever met someone you just knew was different from everyone else? Maybe you remembered that person as humorous, carefree, or extremely positive. Or in your case, maybe you stand out because you do an extraordinary job of making a difference in the lives of others. Whatever makes you memorable and authentically you, embrace it and bring it out in everything you do.

Your presence could incorporate things such as your voice; the amount of energy you portray; your wardrobe; how you groom your hair, your makeup, or your beard; or even the way you stand. Are you polite, friendly, and welcoming? Do you greet others with a smile? These traits trigger trust, opening up the person opposite you to what you have to say. Even a handshake or fist bump tell the other person what your personality type is. You can portray confidence by looking someone in the eye and making sure you have a firm, strong grip while shaking his or her hand or giving a fist bump.

Remember when you walk into a room to feel the atmosphere of the room and adjust. If the person you are meeting gets straight to the point, they most likely do not have time for small talk. If they give off a more relaxed *Vibe*, then work to find something to talk about that's relatable for you and that the person may relate to. Attention to all these social nuances make an impression.

In today's world, your presence could even include the way you present yourself on Zoom. Are you making sure you look sharp, even though you're working from home? What is your backdrop? Often, people are not as strategic as they could be about that, and they may get a little sloppy. For example, they may be wearing a baseball hat or have something in the background that detracts from their presence. As a leader, thinking through all that and being strategic about it can have an impact on your *Vibe*.

IN TODAY'S WORLD, YOUR PRESENCE COULD INCLUDE THE WAY YOU PRESENT YOURSELF ON *ZOOM*.

Choose your wardrobe each day according to what you're going to be doing or who you will be seeing. You may even wear boots that lift your height another inch and a half if you know that extra height will give you a win. If you are meeting a younger person, tennis shoes may be appropriate. Constantly think about what to wear to enhance your presence—and *Vibe*.

Remember, you have just seven seconds to make a great first impression, whether virtually or in person. You want to make sure everything about you is sending a message that your persona is a memorable *Vibe* enhancer.

For the Organization: First Impression

As an organization, one of the best ways to make an excellent first impression is to demonstrate your ability to execute. Within minutes after a meeting at your company, have a follow-up email in the inbox of all the participants with the notes taken during the meeting, along with the audio recording of the meeting.

Your first impression starts before the meeting. A standard operating procedure should be to text people to remind them when you have a meeting scheduled. Send out the meeting agenda ahead of time. These two things will enhance your *Vibe*.

YOUR FIRST IMPRESSION STARTS BEFORE THE MEETING. SENDING OUT MEETING REMINDERS AND THE AGENDA AHEAD OF TIME ENHANCES YOUR *VIBE*.

For example, we have someone coming in to our studio for the first time this afternoon, for the main purpose of meeting another person. So we sent a text to the person we had arranged the meeting for and touched on what the agenda would be, and he sent a text back saying, "Great!" Our first impression with someone new like that was that we are ahead of the game by organizing and confirming the details.

Your organization's physical appearance also impacts the first impression people have of your company, both virtually and in person. When people first sign onto Zoom for our meetings, they see the words "Clarity, Focus, and Execution" (our core methodology) on the wall behind our screen. When they walk into our offices, they see our logo on the door. They see our motto in our foyer: "Give value. Do more than is expected." As they're walking up the stairs to our lounge area, they see the words "Results Faster," along with wall art that validates the fast results we've been able to bring to many of our major clients. All those things make an impression.

We also have a screen in our foyer that displays the name of the clients we are meeting with that day; so when people walk in, one of the first things they see is their name on that screen. That kind of welcome gives a great first impression, and that's an attention to detail that most people either don't think of or don't put the energy into to make it happen.

CREATING AN INNOVATIVE WAY TO WELCOME PEOPLE TO YOUR PLACE OF BUSINESS GIVES A GREAT FIRST IMPRESSION.

When people walk into our studio, we have note tablets at each place with our icon on them, and we have the meeting participants' names on tent cards. All of that lets them know we were expecting them and that they are welcome.

How strategic are you about strengthening your organization's *Vibe* by enhancing the first impression you present?

CHAPTER 23
VIPs

For the Individual Leader: Presence

1. Your *strategic presence* invokes a certain image that causes people to see you as a particular kind of person. Your trademark expression, style, or persona makes you memorable—or not.
2. Whatever makes you memorable and authentically you, embrace it and bring it out in everything you do.
3. As a leader, be strategic about the way you present yourself on Zoom, including what can be seen in your background.
4. Make sure everything about you—including your grooming, your posture, your body language, and even the way you articulate—is sending a message that your persona is a memorable *Vibe* enhancer.

For the Organization: First Impression

5. As an organization, one of the best ways to make an excellent first impression is to demonstrate your ability to execute.
6. Make your first impression one that says you are ahead of the game by organizing and confirming the details.
7. Your organization's physical appearance impacts the first impression people have of your company, both virtually and in person.

CHAPTER 24
HEALTHY/HEALTHY ENVIRONMENT

For the Individual Leader: Healthy

Your *Vibe* is profoundly affected by your health. You can often look at a person and tell how healthy they are. Poor health shows up in a person's skin, their shape, and their vibrance (their energy level). If you want to enhance your *Vibe*, this is a good place to start.

IF YOU WANT TO ENHANCE YOUR *VIBE*, BECOMING HEALTHY IS A VERY IMPORTANT PLACE TO START.

We're currently working on publishing a book for Dr. Scott Conrad, and we started with a small booklet called *Intuitive Health*, which gives twenty-one principles for winning at the game of health. Dr. Scott says:

> I was taught in medical school that your DNA (genes) defined how your body worked and the health challenges that would eventually lead to your death. Knowing what was in your DNA would tell us what we needed to watch for with your health. *We had it backwards!* While some conditions do run in families and there are important genetic conditions, the choices a person makes determine which part of their DNA is "turned on" and the medical conditions that will manifest in their body.
>
> Your DNA *actually responds to your choices, your lifestyle.* For instance, you may have one set of genes to get diabetes and another set to not get diabetes. If you eat certain foods, are sedimentary, and don't get enough sleep consistently, the "diabetes" genes get activated, and you have severe diabetes in middle age. If you choose other foods, are active, and sleep well, you may not develop diabetes until your 80s or 90s.

The point is, *you have tremendous power over how well and how long you live.* All of us set ourselves up for success or for failure through our choices.

You are unique and everyone has different DNA, lifestyle habits, microbiomes, and social interactions. These all influence your health and wellbeing. Only by exploring what works for you in the context of your body's "report card" (for instance your Seven Numbers) can you discover the right path for you . . . I don't believe there is only one "right" way for everyone. In contrast, I believe you have choices and your body responds in unique and different ways that can be observed and appreciated. Your choices matter—to you, to your friends, to those who love you.[5]

YOUR DNA, LIFESTYLE, HABITS, MICROBIOMES, AND SOCIAL INTERACTIONS ALL INFLUENCE YOUR HEALTH AND WELLBEING.

We believe your journey to good health starts with understanding your body. In my book *Ultimate Health* (published in 2013), we included an assessment covering twenty areas that can have the most impact on your health, and we've included that assessment below. This assessment is the first step toward discovering the areas in which you need to improve in order to live in ultimate health and present your best *Vibe.*

ULTIMATE HEALTH ASSESSMENT

Rate yourself on a scale of 1 to 5, with 5 being the highest, on your current effectiveness in each area.

#	Category	Description	Rating
1.	Lifestyle	How are you living your life? Managing balance, managing risks, resting, saying "no" enough, and exercising all make up your overall living routine. Are your habits supporting your health?	
2.	Mental Management	What goes on in our minds truly impacts our health. Assess your own self-talk, your daily attitude, and your beliefs about being healthy and not getting sick; your willingness to release grudges and forgive, while focusing on the positives. Filter the input you receive from sources such as news, media, or even negative people.	
3.	Ultimate Longevity	Do you have a great team of health professionals who know you and guide you? Family doctor? Nutritionist? Dentist? Do you have regular checkups and vaccines? Do your behaviors align with real health?	
4.	Stress Management	Are you managing anxiety? Are you meditating? Relaxing enough? Is your life aligned with your values? Have you set up harmony in your life so things run as smoothly as possible? Is your pace of life contributing to or detracting from your overall wellbeing?	
5.	Immune System	Your immune system protects you. It detects potential harm and helps your body react. Are you helping yourself? Are you resting at the right time, for example, when you sense your body needs it to ensure you stay well? Are you maintaining good hygiene; protecting against harmful bacteria; practicing plain and simple cleanliness, such as washing your hands enough and avoiding being in contact with the wrong things in order to support your wellness?	
6.	Testing	Early detection is great common sense in today's world of information. How is your discipline on staying current on screenings, blood work reviews, EKGs, MRIs, hormone testing, and urinalysis—even full-body skin screenings every few years? There are many simple things we can do to be proactive. Are you taking advantage of these options?	
7.	Exercise	Physical exercise matters—regular, frequent, and ongoing. Resistance exercise, cardiovascular exercise (aerobics), balance, and stretching all promote a better-operating body.	

#	Category	Description	Rating
8.	Oral	Obviously, it is important to keep your mouth clean. Are you brushing enough? Flossing enough? Going for regular check-ups?	
9.	Eyes/Vision	Are you protecting your eyes from sunlight and eating the things that help prevent cataracts later in life? Are you going for regular checkups? Do you wear eye protection when doing certain types of work around the house? All these factors add up to promoting this key component to your body's overall health.	
10.	Toxin Management	What's around you can get in your body through your skin, what you breathe, and what you eat. Toxins are potentially hazardous substances that can place an extra toll on your body, such as forcing your liver and kidneys to work overtime as they filter fluids. Are you protecting yourself like you could or should?	
11.	Hormone Management	A hormone is a chemical released by a cell or a gland in one part of your body that sends out messages that affect cells in other parts of your body. In essence, it's a chemical messenger that transports a signal from one cell to another. Have you tested your chemical balances (estrogen, testosterone, thyroid, DHEA, etc.)? Are you supplementing where you should?	
12.	Vitamins	A vitamin is an organic compound required as a vital nutrient in tiny amounts by an organism. Vitamins help your body function optimally. Are you managing your regular intake, testing so you know, and living daily with the right balances in your body?	
13.	Caloric Management	A calorie is a unit of energy. It is a measure of the energy we generate with every task we do, as well as a measure of the energy delivered by a food we eat. How well do you know your body and how how well you balance what you eat versus what you need to perform? Being in tune and knowing this can allow you to make better daily choices . . . and live better!	
14.	Ear, Nose, and Throat	Preventive testing is important for the ear, nose, and throat, the same as for the rest of your body. It is important to protect your hearing and ear canal from foreign objects and loud noises. Are you maintaining good hygiene? Are you getting checked regularly?	

#	Category	Description	Rating
15.	Food	Food is any substance consumed to provide nutritional support for your body. It is usually of plant or animal origin, and contains essential nutrients, such as carbohydrates, fats, proteins, vitamins, and minerals. It is what we consume in an effort to produce energy, maintain life, and stimulate growth. How is your balance? How is your mix? Are you eating throughout the day to promote good metabolism? Do you eat slowly and chew well in order to promote good digestion? Do you make healthy choices such as limiting the fried, processed, and high-sugar foods you eat?	
16.	Skin	Your skin is the largest organ in your body. It acts as an external filter and can even provide many clues about the condition of your body internally. Are you protecting it like you should from ultraviolet rays or from harmful chemicals that can get into your body? Do you get full body skin screenings to detect cancers or other harmful things that need attention in order to ensure your ultimate health? Skin cancer is the most common cancer there is.	
17.	Fluids	Consuming adequate amounts of water is critical to maintaining ultimate health. Do you drink enough water each day? Do you manage your alcohol intake? Do you drink too much soda or other high-sugar drinks?	
18.	Emotions	Emotion is a complex psychophysiological experience of your state of mind as you interact with internal and external influences. How are your mood, temperament, personality, disposition, and motivation? All these elements matter; all impact the way our bodies perform.	
19.	Sleep	Sleep suspends the sensory activity of nearly all voluntary muscles. It accentuates the growth and rejuvenation of the immune, nervous, skeletal, and muscular systems. Are you getting enough sleep? Is it good sleep?	
20.	Spiritual wellness	Your spiritual wellness is to a large degree reflective of your worldview. Is it egocentric or others oriented? Would others say you display stress tolerance and adequate marginal reserves for life's challenges? What wisdom do you apply to your life situations in order to achieve spiritual balance, peace and joy?	

Your Total: ____________

Interpreting Your Total

A 100 is exceptional—and exceptionally rare. This is not designed to be a scientific assessment, but an awareness tool.

5–20: Red flag
21–55: Average
56–80: Above average
80–100: Excellent

We believe you must be strategic about your health and get clear on who you want to become, then build your health goals and actions around that vision. Take charge of your health and take action in the areas in which you need to improve. Health is a superstructure upon which success, and quality of life rest. You simply cannot have great *Vibe* without great health.

YOU CANNOT HAVE GREAT *VIBE* WITHOUT GREAT HEALTH.

For the Organization: Healthy Environment

How health-minded is your organization? How much value do you place on the health and wellness of your people? Do you realize that healthy employees are more energetic, happier, more innovative, and even more productive?

HOW HEALTH-MINDED IS YOUR ORGANIZATION?

Making your workplace healthier is beneficial for everyone. It adds an incredible *Vibe* that serves to attract many of the A Players of today, and it even improves your bottom line. In fact, a study by the *Harvard Business Review* found that for every dollar invested in wellness, companies average a return of $2.71 by way of increased productivity, decreased absenteeism, and reduced healthcare cost.[6]

Even with many people working from home, when one person is too sick to work, that means that one valuable piece of the puzzle is missing; with too many missing pieces, you lose the complete picture.

If you have a break room for your people, do you provide healthy snacks there or have them in your vending machines? If you serve food, is it healthy? Do you have a clean environment?

DO YOU PROVIDE HEALTHY SNACKS FOR YOUR EMPLOYEES IN YOUR BREAK ROOM AND/OR VENDING MACHINES?

How do you motivate your people to lead a healthy lifestyle? Do you educate them on how to make healthy choices? One way you could do that is by encouraging them to take the health assessment we included in the first section of this chapter so they can become aware of how effective they are in the twenty areas of health we assess. Another idea is to post health-minded posters or notes in your break room. We've developed a deck of health-related reminder cards, and that's something you could put into your break room as well.

ENCOURAGE YOUR EMPLOYEES TO TAKE THE HEALTH ASSESSMENT PROVIDED ABOVE SO THEY CAN BECOME AWARE OF HOW EFFECTIVE THEY ARE IN MAINTAINING THEIR HEALTH.

Creating a *Vibe* that says, "We place a high priority on keeping our team members healthy" will help you achieve your goals and get the results you're looking for.

CHAPTER 24
VIPs

For the Individual: Healthy

1. Your *Vibe* is profoundly affected by your health.
2. You have tremendous power over how well and how long you live. All of us set ourselves up for success or for failure through our choices.
3. Taking the health assessment in this chapter is the first step toward discovering the areas in which you need to improve in order to live in ultimate health and present your best *Vibe*.
4. Be strategic about your health and get clear on who you want to become, and then build your health goals and actions around that vision.

For the Organization: Healthy Environment

5. Making your workplace healthier is beneficial for everyone. It adds an incredible *Vibe* that serves to attract many of the A Players of today, and it even improves your bottom line.
6. It's important to motivate your people to lead a healthy lifestyle and educate them on how to make healthy choices.
7. Creating a *Vibe* that says, "We place a high priority on keeping our team members healthy" will help you achieve your goals and get the results you're looking for.

CHAPTER 25
HAPPY/FUN

For the Individual Leader: Happy

A happy person emits a positive *Vibe*.

In 2018 I coauthored a book called *Living Life Smiling* with my great friend and business partner Dr. Daryl Holmes, founder and owner of a large dental group in Australia. In the book we talk about the difference between happiness and joy. Both are positive emotions that are satisfying in nature, yet many people don't give much thought to the big difference between the two. Happiness is an emotion and is temporary and mostly dependent upon outside circumstances; joy is an attitude of the heart. You can be both joyful and happy at the same time; and yet just because you are happy, it doesn't mean you are joyful.

Joy is an inner peace that is present despite your circumstances. Joy can be described as a wonderful feeling in the soul (mind, will, and emotions), and is a God-given condition of the heart. It is a settled state of contentment, confidence, and hope grounded in an appreciation of life's blessings.

Happiness is a feeling of pleasure or contentment that is externally triggered by a pleasant experience and/or environment, and it is often based on other people, things, places, thoughts, and events. Joy is more consistent and is cultivated internally. It comes when you make peace with who you are and your purpose in life. You actually have control over both joy and happiness in your life.

JOY IS AN INNER PEACE THAT IS PRESENT DESPITE YOUR CIRCUMSTANCES. HAPPINESS IS A FEELING OF PLEASURE OR CONTENTMENT THAT IS EXTERNALLY TRIGGERED BY A PLEASANT EXPERIENCE AND/OR ENVIRONMENT.

People often use *joy* and *happiness* interchangeably. For the purpose of this chapter, we will stick with the most often used term, *happiness*.

In *Living Life Smiling*, we address five key areas of life that are critical to finding and living a life of happiness. These five areas create the acronym SMILE—Significance, Money, Inspiration, Lifestyle, and Engagement—and then we add another "S" at the end, because all of them together equal Success.

S Significance: doing what is most meaningful and what matters the most to you

M Money: enjoying cash flow, financial freedom, and giving back to others

I Inspiration: having positive emotions and a state of mind that inspires motivation

L Lifestyle: living a happy life that includes good habits and intentional actions

E Engagement: being immersed in work and people you love, and enjoying others

=

S **SUCCESS:** living with purpose and alignment, and ensuring that others win!

In the book, we include a "Happiness Index" that allows you to gain perspective and awareness of where you are in each of these areas. We suggest you get a copy of the book and take that assessment; then take it again after you have read through the book and see how much you have increased your score by changing some of your thinking and putting into place many of the ideas we present.

We believe living a life that is congruent with your values and living your life's purpose actually form the foundation for the happiness we describe. Many people get so busy *doing* life that they don't take the time to step back and make sure the life they are doing is impacting others, is significant, and—perhaps most importantly—is aligned with their values.

We propose that in order to truly be happy and emit the kind of *Vibe* that will make you the best leader you can be, you need to get clarity on your values, list them, and then align them with your daily activities.

IN ORDER TO TRULY BE HAPPY AND EMIT THE KIND OF *VIBE* THAT WILL MAKE YOU THE BEST LEADER YOU CAN BE, YOU NEED TO GET CLARITY ON YOUR VALUES, LIST THEM, AND THEN ALIGN THEM WITH YOUR DAILY ACTIVITIES.

We've developed a comprehensive list of things people value. Even though you may relate to many items on the list, we encourage you to choose the ten that represent what you value the most so you can intentionally focus on those things that bring the most meaning to your life. Circle those top ten in the list.

1. Affection
2. Alignment
3. Altruism
4. Appearance
5. Appreciated
6. Attitude
7. Cleanliness
8. Congruence
9. Contentment
10. Cooperation
11. Creativity
12. Education
13. Effectiveness
14. Efficiency
15. Fairness
16. Faith
17. Fame
18. Family
19. Financial Security
20. Freedom
21. Friendship
22. Fun
23. Generosity
24. Genuineness
25. Happiness
26. Harmony
27. Health
28. Honesty
29. Humility
30. Inner Peace
31. Inspiration
32. Intimacy
33. Joy
34. Knowledge
35. Lifestyle
36. Loved
37. Loyalty
38. Motivation
39. Openness
40. Organization
41. Personal Brand
42. Personal Improvement
43. Personal Salvation
44. Philanthropy
45. Power
46. Productivity
47. Recognition
48. Respect
49. Results
50. Romance
51. Routine
52. Security
53. See the World
54. Simplicity
55. Solitude
56. Spiritual Maturity
57. Status
58. Wealth
59. Winning
60. Wisdom

Gratitude, the quality of being thankful and the readiness to show appreciation for and return kindness, plays a big role in your happiness and therefore in your *Vibe*. The benefits of practicing gratitude are nearly endless. Gratefulness—and especially the expression of it to others—is associated with increased energy, optimism, and empathy. People who regularly practice gratitude by taking time to notice and reflect upon the things they're thankful for exude a tremendous amount of *Vibe*. They experience more positive emotions, feel more alive, sleep better, express more compassion and kindness, and even have stronger immune systems.

Happiness is the sum of many small things, and being grateful for the simple things is important for creating happiness. We recommend keeping a gratitude journal—especially on your phone—adding to it often, and reflecting and praying over it frequently. We believe it will positively impact your life—and your *Vibe*.

For the Organization: Fun

How important is fun in your organization's culture?

According to humorthatworks.com, "People who use humor at work are more productive, less stressed, and happier, so it's no surprise that using humor and having fun is an important part of a strong company culture."[7] Many organizations include "fun" as a core value because they know it plays a major part not only in keeping their employees happy, but also in enhancing the *Vibe* of their brand.

HOW IMPORTANT IS FUN IN YOUR ORGANIZATION'S CULTURE?

How serious are you in your meetings? One of the things I do is give away crisp brand new dollar bills to encourage people to smile and make witty remarks so people will enjoy our meetings more. If you have your meetings buttoned up so you are clear on what your objectives are, then it's easy to include a little fun factor so you can get that spike of energy. When people are laughing, it exudes a powerful *Vibe* and synergy.

WHEN PEOPLE ARE LAUGHING, IT EXUDES A POWERFUL *VIBE* AND SYNERGY.

There are many ways you can create an atmosphere of fun in your culture. It can be as simple as playing fun, upbeat music in the background or showing funny videos in your staff meetings (we have an entire arsenal of them, which you can request by writing to us at info@tonyjeary.com). And you can add to the fun factor by encouraging camaraderie in your organization, along with ownership and transparency. An atmosphere of fun builds teamwork and trusting relationships. People enjoy the opportunity to work together to help drive the growth of your business. A culture of fun often produces team members who are mentally and emotionally healthy, and they in turn usually produce the most satisfied customers. And be sure to celebrate wins—often. People love to be recognized and rewarded for their work. Celebrate milestones for individuals, teams, and the company as a whole—and be sure to make the celebrations fun.

A CULTURE OF FUN OFTEN PRODUCES EMPLOYEES WHO ARE MENTALLY AND EMOTIONALLY HEALTHY, AND THEY, IN TURN, USUALLY PRODUCE THE MOST SATISFIED CUSTOMERS.

There are many wins from having an organization that promotes the fun factor. Nonstop work and no play will likely produce dissatisfied people and less productivity, while empowering employees to have fun creates a happier and healthier team, a much more enticing *Vibe*, and an increased bottom line.

CHAPTER 25
VIPs

For the Individual Leader: Happy

1. A happy person emits a positive *Vibe.*
2. Happiness is an emotion and is temporary, mostly dependent upon outside circumstances; joy is an attitude of the heart. You actually have control over both joy and happiness in your life. (We use the word *happiness* for both in this chapter.)
3. We believe there are five key areas of life that are critical to finding and living a life of happiness: significance, money, inspiration, lifestyle, and engagement and that together, these result in Success.
4. Living a life that is congruent with your values and living your life's purpose actually form the foundation for your happiness.
5. People who regularly practice gratitude by taking time to notice and reflect upon the things they're thankful for exude a tremendous amount of *Vibe.*

For the Organization: Fun

6. A culture of fun often produces team members who are mentally and emotionally healthy, and they in turn usually produce the most satisfied customers.
7. If you have your meetings buttoned up so you are clear on what your objectives are, then it's easy to include a little fun factor so you can get that spike of energy. When people are laughing, it exudes a powerful *Vibe* and synergy.
8. Nonstop work and no play will likely produce a dissatisfied team and less productivity, while empowering people to have fun creates happier and healthier people, a much more enticing *Vibe*, and an increased bottom line.

CONCLUSION

Our entire message throughout this book has been that energy, *Vibe*, is a supercharger—a *force multiplier*—for every facet of your life, whether you're an individual who leads yourself and/or your family, you're a leader of a small or large team, or you're the leader of an entire organization. We hope you've absorbed what we've shared in the book and are asking yourself, *Am I intentionally bringing energy to my world?*

Now that you've been exposed to what we've shared, are you ready to double down on being strategic about bringing energy to a room, to your life, to your brand, to your personality, or to your entire organization? We believe people who are intentional about improving their *Vibe* think better; have better relationships; are better leaders because they're more caring, more efficient, and more organized; and they are healthier and happier. If that's what you want, it's up to you—on a daily and even an hourly basis—to put forth the effort. You may be a person it comes naturally to, or maybe you realize you need to work to tune up your *Vibe* a little more.

Things you do to enhance your *Vibe* can often be the result of an impromptu decision, and/or it could be done as the result of a longer-term decision, where you prepare ahead. When your *Vibe* is top of mind, you're ready for any event. We've presented ideas and scenarios in this book to hopefully help you plan ahead more and make decisions that will steadily increase your *Vibe* little by little as you live your life.

Daniel and I agree that one thing is sure: *Vibe* is a difference-maker. To some people, this concept is actually an *aha* or even an *epiphany*. If you're one who is already aware of it, we hope you're going to be more refined in what you do as a result of what you've read. As we continue to say, don't be a squatter (a person who doesn't do squat when they know they're supposed to do something). We urge you to be more intentional because the *why* is a giant payoff. When you emit a powerful *Vibe*, the people who are connected to you want to be around you, more opportunities come to you, you light up a room, and you get more thank-you notes, more appreciation, more of everything.

As Daniel and I work side by side together, we are looking at how we make decisions about the environment of our office so it has *Vibe*. We make decisions about the entrance, our video, what people will see as they walk into our office, and even what we're going to say. In our meetings with clients, we consider whether we should pivot during a conversation and facilitate other people talking more. We're constantly having discussions on how we can sharpen our own *Vibe* because we believe it's such a powerful strategic asset.

Throughout this book, we've given examples of how you can create the kind of *Vibe* you want. If you want to have *Vibe* in your personal brand by being known as a person who gives attention to detail, maybe you need to improve your habit of making lists and determine to get things done without offering excuses. Life is not perfect, so sometimes we just have to plow through it.

Daniel and I both believe a great part of our *Vibe* is our being intentional in making sure other people win. In fact, our shared passion is to help those we connect with win—in their world, in their situation, in their capacity, and in their priorities. That's why we're excited to bring you this book. We want you to win in everything you do, and we hope we've poured enough of our own *Vibe* into you through this book that we have stimulated your thinking, energized you, and created the momentum you need to achieve a *Vibe* that will change your life.

Now, take the following assessment and evaluate where you are in terms of *Vibe* in all twenty-five areas that we've discussed. If you need to improve in any of the areas, go back and study the appropriate chapters and determine to grow your *Vibe* so you can be your very best.

THE *VIBE* ASSESSMENT

#	Leadership/Individual	Rate 1-4	Organization/Team	Rate 1-4
		Brand		
1.	Open and growing (open, listening, and caring)		Innovative (ex: bringing in outside expertise)	
2.	Wardrobe (first impression)		Environment (Vibe, current design, and MO)	
3.	LinkedIn or Wiki (what people find)		Website and Reviews (what people find)	
4.	Accomplishments (what have you done?)		Customer Testimonials (what do customers say your company has done?)	
5.	Attitude (supportive, caring)		Caring (supportive)	
		Leadership		
6.	Goals (written personal goals, vision board)		Mission, Vision, Strategic Objectives (cascaded and referred to often)	
7.	Discipline (know where you're going and staying on the path)		Standards (posted, shared in onboarding)	
8.	Team Player (accountable, communicative, and trustworthy)		*High-Performing Team* (HPT) (accountability, communication, and trust)	
9.	Clarity and Focus		Clarity and Focus	
10.	Flexible		Bureaucracy (vs. streamlined, efficient)	
		Organization		
11.	Efficient		Best-Practice Oriented	
12.	Organized		Everything in Order	
13.	Arsenal (tools to make you better and that you can share with your team)		Tool Chest (tools you can share with your team)	
14.	Life Team (people who help you be the best you can be [CPA, plumbers, hairstylist, etc.])		Company Team (A Players)	
15.	Energized		Fast Paced	

(continued on next page)

#	Leadership/Individual	Rate 1-4	Organization/Team	Rate 1-4
		Communication		
16.	Presentations (outlined, with objectives, what, why, how, and time; rehearsed)		Meetings (with objectives and great agenda; efficient)	
17.	Listening		Speaking (taking opportunities to promote company's brand, internally and externally)	
18.	Timely, Prepared		Ahead with News and Direction	
19.	Always Improving		Sharpening the Communication Saw	
20.	Emailing and Texting (short, sweet, and to the point, with great subject and bullets)		Emailing and Style (training for email efficiency)	
		Style		
21.	Buttoned Up and Prepared (*planned spontaneity*)		Everything in Place	
22.	Calm		Peaceful	
23.	Presence (positive impression, influence)		First impression (positive vibe)	
24.	Healthy		Healthy Environment	
25.	Happy		Fun	

ABOUT THE AUTHORS

Tony Jeary, known as The RESULTS Guy™, is a strategist, thought leader, and prolific author of over sixty titles, multiple best sellers, and hundreds of courses. Tony is unique and sought after by the world's best. His client list has now exceeded one thousand organizations in over fifty countries. He truly is a special resource that delivers and is a "secret weapon" to many business savvy leaders.

Tony was raised by entrepreneurial parents and grandparents who thrived on identifying and pursuing new opportunities to serve others. His father taught him the powerful principle that has driven Tony's professional and personal life: "Always give more than is expected." As a result, exceeded expectations is the common thread that every Tony Jeary client experiences firsthand.

For more than two decades, Tony has advised the world's top CEOs, entrepreneurs, and other high achievers on how to discover new clarity for their vision, develop focus on their direction, and create powerful execution strategies that impact achievement and results. He personally coaches the most accomplished people in the world, including presidents of: Walmart, Sam's Club, Ford, American Airlines, HP, Firestone, Samsung, and New York Life.

When many top achievers seek a strategic expert to help them accelerate their results, they are eventually drawn to Tony. He is the authority on RESULTS and has committed his career to studying and helping others think better and achieve more. His specialty is compressed time, meaning he delivers "vision to reality" in time frames many can't even believe—both virtually and in person.

Tony has been described as a "gifted encourager" who facilitates positive outcomes for others. His list of personal and professional relationships numbers in the area of 40,000, and he connects with and nourishes these relationships out of his sincere interest in and desire for shared success.

Tony has personal experience with both success and failure. He made and lost millions before he reached the age of thirty. That early experience with failure propelled him to help others live smart, live on purpose, and be their very best. Today, he walks the talk and practices the distinctions that characterize success, both personally and professionally, encouraging others to think strategically about everything.

Tony lives and works in the Dallas/Fort Worth area where at his brand-new think tank, the RESULTS Center, he and his hand-picked team strategically assemble powerful game plans, inspire high performance, and encourage all those he touches, resulting in enhanced sales/profits, and raising companies' value. *info@tonyjeary.com*

ABOUT THE AUTHORS

Daniel Marold is Tony's protégé and currently serves as the publisher for RESULTS Faster Publishing and the COO of Tony Jeary International. He brings his fifteen years of international presentation and servant leadership expertise to the dynamic.

Before joining Tony, Daniel served as CEO at his family business, Bohlin, a high-end accessories company that caters to the same niche of high-performing clientele. He also taught a series of leadership and communication courses in China, parts of Europe, and all across the United States.

Daniel has worked closely with Tony for three years to lead others to greatness. During those three years, he has developed a public dental campaign for 1300SMILES in Western Australia, all the while managing operations, building relationships, and shaping stories for publishing to match the authors' objectives.

WHAT WE CAN DO FOR YOU

RESULTS Coaching

Advice Matters, if it's the right advice. Having coached the world's top CEOs, published over forty books, and advised over one thousand clients, Tony has positioned himself with a unique track record to take serious high achievers to a whole new level of results.

Interactive Keynotes

Tony not only energizes, entertains, and educates; he also has his team work strategically and smartly with the event team to make his part as well as the entire experience a super win. An hour with Tony often changes people's lives forever and impacts an organization's results immediately. He delivers value, a fun factor, and best practices people can really use.

Strategic Acceleration Facilitation Planning

Tony can do in a single day what takes many others days and even weeks to accomplish. He has refined a process so powerful the world travels to his private think tank (called the RESULTS Center) to experience clarity, focus, and the ability to synergistically execute. He provides at your fingertips two decades of best practices, processes, and tools for accelerating dramatic, sustained results in any organization.

Collaborative Relationships

We selectively partner with organizations in a *Growth Partnership* arrangement. We supercharge and help winners win more. Most winning leaders know they can always win better and faster teaming up with the right people, adding the right resources and becoming more clear on their vision. Our foundational methodology of Clarity, Focus and

Execution is deployed in such a way that our partners get the right RESULTS Faster.

We built a multi-million dollar think tank that is seven minutes from the DFW Airport, called the RESULTS Center that is the ultimate destination where teams synergize, powerful plans are built, and individuals become energized to compress their time to turn visions into reality—often in less time than believed possible.

We have over 30,000 contacts, 3 decades of proprietary built tools, multiple investment options, a hand selected team and a 30-year proven track record, all to be leveraged with the right partners. We bring energy (*Vibe*) to the table.

Please visit **tonyjeary.com** as well as **tonyjearytheresultsguy.com** and then reach out and discuss what we can do for you.

ENDNOTES

1 Dee Edington, "Caring is a Shared Value of Employees and Organization," Core Health Workplace Wellness Blog, March 12, 2018, accessed 7/28/20, www.blog.corehealth.global.

2 Gary Hamel and Michele Zanini, "What We Learned About Bureaucracy from 7,000 HBR Readers," August 10, 2017, accessed 8/14/20, https://hbr.org/2017/08/what-we-learned-about-bureaucracy-from-7000-hbrreaders#:~:text=A%20survey%20of%20more%20than,matters%20rather%20than%20their%20customers.

3 Harper & Hill, https://harperandhill.com/executive-search/the-workplace-future-creating-a-peaceful-work-environment/, accessed 12/8/2020.

4 Harper & Hill, https://harperandhill.com/executive-search/the-workplace-future-creating-a-peaceful-work-environment/, accessed 12/8/2020.

5 Scott Conard, Intuitive Wellbeing passport (Dallas, RESULS Faster Publishing, 2020).

6 https://snacknation.com/blog/corporate-wellness-companies/, accessed 12/12/20.

7 https://www.humorthatworks.com/how-to/fun-as-a-core-value/ (accessed 12/14/20).